The Exporter's Handbook to the U.S. Wine Market

THE EXPORTER'S HANDBOOK TO THE U.S. WINE MARKET

DEBORAH M. GRAY

The Exporter's Handbook to the U.S. Wine Market
Text copyright © 2015 Deborah M. Gray

Wine Appreciation Guild
an imprint of
Board and Bench Publishing
www.boardandbench.com

No part of this publication may be reproduced, distributed, or transmitted in any form or by any means, including photocopying, recording, or other electronic or mechanical methods, without the prior written permission of the publisher.

Editor: Judith Chien
Book design and composition: TIPS Technical Publishing, Inc.
Cover design: Tijana Mihajlovic

Library of Congress Cataloging-in-Publication Data

Gray, Deborah M.
  The exporter's handbook to the U.S. wine market / Deborah M. Gray.
    1 online resource.
  Includes index.
  Description based on print version record and CIP data provided by publisher; resource not viewed.
  ISBN 978-1-935879-54-1 (pdf) — ISBN 978-1-935879-53-4 (epub) — ISBN 978-1-935879-55-8
  1. Wine industry—United States. 2. Exports—United States. 3. Wine and wine making—United States—Marketing. 4. Business logistics—United States. I. Title.
  HD9375
  663'.200688—dc23
                         2015034730

Although all reasonable care has been taken in the preparation of this book, neither the author nor the publisher can accept liability for any consequences arising from the information contained herein or from use thereof.

Printed and bound in the U.S.A.

*To Grant, Tyler and Zachary
and Catherine Gray*

Contents

Acknowledgments   xi
Introduction   xiii

Part I

1. **Understanding the U.S. Market**..3
   Top Ten Myths and Misconceptions   3
   Current Influences on the U.S. Wine Industry   8
   An Overview of the U.S. Wine Industry   10
   Fifty Different States—A Potpourri of Cultures   13
   Final Thoughts   14

2. **Breaking Down the States** 15
   Top Ten Wine States by Volume   15
   Per Capita Consumption   16
   Alcoholic Beverage Control and Franchise States   17
   Final Thoughts   20

3. **U.S. Importing Alternatives** 21
   Setting up Your Own Import Company   21
   Selling To An Independent Importer   23
   Setting up a Hybrid Supplier-Importer Business   24
   Appointing a Compliance Importer   26
   Final Thoughts   26

4. **A Role Defined** 29
   Importer as Gatekeeper   29
   Top Ten Things to Look for in a U.S. Importer   34
   How to Find an Importer   37
   Trade Shows and Wine Fairs   40
   Foreign Trade Organizations   44
   Internet Website Search   46
   Wine Brands—Reverse Importer Search   47
   LinkedIn   48
   Other Connections   50
   Final Thoughts   51

5. **Exploring Options** 53
   An Export Broker/Agent   54
   Awards, Medals, Ratings   56
   Cellar Door Visits   57
   Final Thoughts   59

Part II

6. **The Courtship** 63
   Narrowing the Field   63
   The Personalities   63
   Expectations—Yours and Theirs   65
   Background Checking   71
   Final Thoughts   71

7. **The Engagement** 73
   Samples   73
   FDA Registrations   75
   Contracts   77
   Sample Allowance   78
   Payment Currency   80
   Pricing—In Brief   81
   Short-Term Goals   81
   Final Thoughts   82

8. **The Commitment** 85
   American Source Letter   85
   COLA (Certificate of Label Approval)   89

Purchase Orders   97
Marketing and POS Material   99
Final Thoughts   106

9. **Logistics** 107
Payment Terms   108
Shipping Terminology and Regulations   109
Freight Forwarder   112
Consolidations   113
Prior Notice   114
Invoice, Packing Slip, Bill of Lading   114
Final Thoughts   118

10. **A Meeting of the Minds** 119
Pricing—In Depth   119
Positioning   124
Brand Launch   125
Final Thoughts   128

Part III

11. **A Long Distance Relationship** 131
Vetting the Distributor   131
Brokers   132
Sample Usage—Publications   134
Sample Usage—Pre-Selling   136
Sample Usage—Wholesaler/Distributor   138
Incentives   139
Communication   143
Final Thoughts   145

12. **Keeping the Momentum Going** 147
Supporting Short Term Goals   147
Market Visit Timing   148
Planning The Trip   152
Budget   156
Paving the Way   157
Final Thoughts   161

13. **On the Road** **163**
    Protocol   164
    Local Customs   165
    Outreach   167
    Events   169
    Trade Tastings   172
    Results   175
    Final Thoughts   178

14. **Thinking Outside the Box** **179**
    Retail Chains   180
    Private Labels   182
    Cruise Ships   184
    Final Thoughts   185

15. **In for the Long Haul** **189**
    Staying Ahead of Demand   189
    Vintage Management   191
    Reorder Timing   192
    Long Term Goal Planning   193
    Social Media   194
    Final Thoughts   198

Conclusion   201
Foreign Trade Organizations   203
Index   205

Acknowledgments

Since the publication of my last book in 2011, I have been fortunate to receive many emails and kind words from readers who approached the book either as an exercise to determine their level of interest in the wine industry, or were in the throes of a new import business and used it as a guide. I am grateful to them for their feedback, because it gave me the courage and inspiration to write another.

Daily, my diverse consulting clients keep me on my toes and abreast of the latest regulations, industry developments and trends, among other things. It is often in the resolution of their issues that I add to my own storehouse of knowledge as a consultant and a writer.

Many thanks to Bryan Imelli, of Board and Bench Publishing.

Love and gratitude to my husband, Grant, and my boys, Tyler and Zachary, who take it for granted that I will keep on writing and support me every step of the way. And special recognition of my sister, Catherine, who once again spent countless hours editing my first drafts, for which I am so appreciative. Any errors that remain are all mine.

Introduction

China is poised to join the top wine consumption countries of the world. This is an extraordinary feat when considering that a few short years ago there was very little wine consumed in China at all, and beer was the alcoholic beverage of choice. China is going through growing pains, but it is currently the new horizon for foreign wine exports, with enormous potential and a burgeoning market for the surplus that has resulted from economic challenges elsewhere. Wineries in Australia, France and the United States have turned their attention to China to either dip their toe in the water, take up their wine glut or in an opportunistic bid to ride a trend. However, as I write this, there are indications that the bubble is about to burst in China for higher end wine. Who knows what will happen in a few months or a year from now.

So what is the relevance of this to exporting wine to the U.S.? This is one example of an evolving world, as it *always has been.* Today is no different. Markets that were once new and exciting are now established, and others are declining. Some, especially in Asia, are developing a greater sophistication or appreciation for wines as their economies, and incomes, rise. Wines and regions are going through their own popularity ebb and flow, independently of everything else.

The United States is the most important market for wine today and looks like being so for the foreseeable future. After passing the French and Italians for largest total wine consumption in 2011, according to *Impact Databank*, Americans consumed 328.7 million cases of wine in 2013. This is again increased from 2012 and caps a decade of double digit growth, despite a crippling recession and lingering aftereffects. Consumption continues to rise, both in terms of population and per capita. The good news for anyone considering exporting to the U.S. is that the age groups known as Millennial and Gen-X (21 to 48 years old) are drinking more imported wine than previous generations. And they are becoming more discriminating. According to Shanken Daily Report, new brands are being launched, aimed at an *"aspirational, yet economically-conscious Millennial audience who are continuing to drive the growth of the popular premium category."*

Since the late 1980s when my father tried twice to export his wines to the U.S., and failed both times with considerable financial loss, I have seen the difficulties of trying to penetrate an unfamiliar market. When the foreign winery has no connections to anyone on the ground and very little understanding of what it takes to find the right connection, the importer will make the difference between success and failure.

In 1992, I started my own U.S. import venture, initially to provide that bridge for my family's wines. I had been living in the United States for several years at that point and although I was not previously in the wine industry, I still seemed to be the best alternative to the dishonest and unprofessional importers my Dad had encountered. Of course, my 'best' was relative in this case. I was completely lacking in experience and I made a lot of early mistakes, but at least my father knew I had his back and I would persevere on his behalf. I eventually took on several other wineries and formed a solid Australian small winery portfolio, but it was a steep and costly learning curve. It was for that reason that I wrote the first book on wine importing, *How to Import Wine—An Insider's Guide*, to help others avoid those pitfalls in the same situation.

Now, as a result of my consulting work, involvement with sites like LinkedIn and people who reach out to me on email, I see that the questions my father had and the confusion he experienced about this market are still being echoed by wineries from all over the world. It has compelled me to focus on the flip side of importing and try to unravel some of the mysteries for exporters who would like an opportunity to sell their wines in the United States. In other words, help you find someone who has your back.

Prior to the start of the recession in 2008, the U.S. was a Mecca for wines from everywhere and many thought this was always going to be the case. The countries whose wines enjoyed enormous acceptance and comfortable sales growth in the U.S. planned their futures with this factor as a constant, and emerging wine brands saw the United States as the marketplace where 300 million people would absorb their tiny production as the ocean might receive a drop of rain. Regions all over the globe expanded their reach, continuing to invest in increased planting, vineyard management and infrastructure, prepared to accelerate wine volume as quickly as demand grew in the U.S.

Ratings were king then, a high U.S. wine publication score the equivalent of anointing a champion, with a winery happily proclaiming, "if you want a bottle of this wine, better decide quickly before it is gone," and it *would* be gone, swallowed up in the frenzy of distributor demand for their "allocation." There was a time when a 90 point rating from a respected wine publication, usually Wine Spectator or The Wine Advocate, guaranteed a sales spike and a 95 point rating would incite a stampede. I knew of U.S. importers who would not place their orders with wineries until the relevant ratings issue had been published and they were assured of winners. In the 1990s, I recall very well where I was when I received news of the first 90 points for a wine I represented. At a wine trade show in Colorado, competitors came up to my booth to congratulate me, knowing the level of sales I could expect from this achievement. Later, when a 90 score was more commonplace, I still found myself in the enviable position of having to severely restrict sales of a limited production, reasonably priced wine that rated 96 in Wine Spectator working from a spreadsheet to allocate case numbers as fairly as possible between multiple distributors and retailers. I am certainly not alone in that experience.

Fast forward to today and a 98 point rating for a premium wine may barely cause a ripple. In the United States, we have entered a vastly different arena, one in which a perfect storm of issues has changed everything:

- Economic constraints through less disposable income and reduced use of credit
- Proliferation of vineyards and regions
- Consolidation of U.S. distributors and investment in their own brands
- Weak U.S. dollar
- Rise of the personal recommendation
- Emphasis on social media and peer influence
- Waning of the subjective ratings system

These have conspired to create a market that is in the process of reinvention. Notice, I didn't say "disintegration" or "decline." The new economic and societal conditions do not negate opportunities for exported wines. It is just not as easy as it once was and the old rules no longer apply. The days of the Wine Gold Rush in the U.S. are over, but gold rushes and the dawn of new eras are always temporary. Nothing stays at a fever pitch forever. Many people strike it rich during those heady times and many others spend their days chasing a pipe dream, unprepared and unable to grasp its wispy smoke before it disappears. The U.S. has become a wine market of changed expectations. Ratings from one or two major wine publications, although still important, no longer monopolize tastes and buying decisions.

The arena is different conditions in other respects. Global communication is far easier and more prolific in a variety of forms, such as Skype and webinars, social media occupies a much more prominent position in the marketing segment and the Millennial generation is changing how, when and what wine is consumed. But wine attributes, diversity, price and packaging are paramount and have supplanted the formerly ratings-driven market, where a wine's appeal was dictated by one or two palates and wineries were pursuing an often nebulous and elusive goal.

We are finally emerging from the recession with steady projected growth in the U.S. and now might very well be the best time for the market savvy, well-positioned winery to enter the fray. It isn't the same world it once was, but learning the new rules makes success feasible. This is where diligence, creativity, perseverance and long term planning play a far bigger role in bringing wines to the U.S. and into the consumer's hands. And sometimes luck, timing and serendipity. But no voyages end up at an intended destination without plotting a course. No new wine export venture into the U.S. can prevail without at least a rudimentary knowledge of this complex market, well before embarking on the first attempt. And for those who have attempted and failed in the past, or found an importer but limped along with varying results, it's time to tear up previous projections and start afresh. The intention of this book is to give a winery owner, vigneron or exporter the navigational tools to steer a course through this market like a seasoned pro.

Part I

1

Understanding the U.S. Market

Top Ten Myths and Misconceptions

When I wrote the book on U.S. wine importing I imagined it would also give the exporter a rare glimpse into the workings of a complex wine market in a country that was often the objective of a foreign winery's aspirations. I believe that most of *How to Import Wine—An Insider's Guide* does just that, but in the time since it was published, I have come to realize that many misconceptions remain. I am faced with the same issues and questions day after day from exporters and foreign (i.e. non-U.S.) wineries that U.S. importers have learned by dealing with it every day, or take for granted as inhabitants of this country.

Therefore, addressing the top ten misconceptions will be the first order of business in this chapter.

#1 The USA is One Market

I have heard this one so many times it deserves top billing on the misconception hit parade. That it persists is understandable. After all, Germany is one market, France is one market, as is each of Australia, New Zealand and so on. In fact, much of Europe can freely trade across country borders. It is inconceivable that one country has fifty different markets, as the U.S. does, along with fifty different sets of rules, laws and regulations, but it is one of the most important factors in distribution here and will be emphasized in other areas of the book.

#2   **Importer, Agent, and Distributor all Mean the Same Thing**
Wineries outside the U.S. are often accustomed to the word "agent" as a person who handles the importation and distribution of wines in their respective markets. This is not a term used at all in the U.S. There is only one entity that a foreign brand owner will sell to and that is a wine importer. To the uninitiated, the term "importer" appears indistinguishable from "distributor" and some foreign producers use it interchangeably. In the U.S., the titles are as different as vigneron is from importer or distributor is from retailer, and must be understood from the outset. That's not to say an importer cannot also be a distributor—under certain circumstances—but to understand the roles, we must look at them in their discrete forms.

Importer is the term for the licensed person or company who directly liaises with the winery (in most instances) and is the only entity authorized to import alcohol into the U.S. An importer is licensed by the Alcohol Tobacco Tax Bureau (TTB) a Federal government agency.

Distributor is the licensed company in a particular state and which is authorized to buy alcohol from an importer and sell it to a retail store, restaurant, hotel, grocery store, casino or chain within their state boundaries. They are also known as a wholesaler or wholesale distributor.

#3   **Anyone From a Foreign Country Can Send Samples at Any Time to Someone in the U.S.**
A foreign supplier can *only* send wine to or through a federally licensed importer. No winery or wine supplier can send wine to a consumer in the U.S., even if the customer paid for it at the point of origin during a vineyard visit, or through a website with a credit card, *unless* they are sending it through the proper channels, that is with COLA (Certificate of Label Approval) or COLA waiver and cleared legally through U.S. Customs. The former is the U.S. compliant label that the importer obtains for the supplier and the latter is an exception for samples. Both issues will be discussed in much more detail in a chapter devoted to conforming U.S. labels.

In this instance I am not referring to unaccompanied wine, i.e. in the luggage of a person traveling from overseas, for whom there is a duty free allowance of one liter per person. In every other circumstance, U.S. Customs prohibits the transit of alcohol, in any amount, via air or ocean, via any commercial carrier, without either a COLA or a COLA waiver. Although these tasks are the purview of the importer, it is incumbent upon the exporter to be apprised of the requirements, so that the samples start their journey within legal parameters. Many people try to 'wing' it or 'game the system,' but to do so invites intervention by U.S. Customs, which will most certainly seize the non-compliant shipment and either destroy it or return it at the exporter's expense. Any importer who tries to have a foreign supplier ship samples in this way also risks their own license.

Besides, although shipping and clearance can be expensive, the process to ship samples is neither onerous nor cost-prohibitive in the pursuit of an importer.

#4 **Only Serious Prospects Request Samples**
I would hope this is true, but of course it isn't always. Any exporter or producer in Europe or the Southern Hemisphere is understandably thinking that only importers who seriously want to consider representation would bother with the nuisance and expense of requesting samples or agreeing to a request from the winery to ship samples.

The cost to clear samples through U.S. Customs is from around $35 to $125, depending upon whether your importer carries a continuous bond, or has to pay a single bond each time a shipment is cleared. It would also depend in part on the number of cases of wine since duty is involved, but this is a nominal amount compared to freight costs. As a rule, the cost of samples and shipping generally falls to the exporter, and the U.S. importer is often responsible for customs clearance.

Most importers are just trying to earn a living, employing reasonable practices and making decisions based on what they think will sell. Obviously, they need to taste the wine they may represent and consider it in context with other factors, such as price and packaging. Determining that you have a serious importer prospect is paramount in determining whether you should send samples. All of this is covered in more detail later.

#5 **Producers Can Sell to any U.S. Wine Business**
You may have a very interested retailer who visits your vineyard and would love to sell your wine in his or her shop, but this is only possible if an importer *and* distributor are also involved in the process. These days, many importers are also distributors and vice versa, and very large retailers use these wholesale arms (importer/distributor) to clear product for them at a nominal cost, but in its simplest form the fact is that a foreign supplier cannot sell to just any U.S. wine business. And even the most enthusiastic

interest from one party, that is distributor, retailer or consumer, cannot guarantee representation in the U.S. market. Only an importer is licensed to bring wines to the U.S. for sale.

#6   Once an Importer Buys the Wine, the Producer has Nothing Else to do

This is probably one of the misconceptions that is most damaging to the wine producer and their relationship with the importer. Although we might all wish otherwise, the purchase is just the start of the transaction. What this means and how to build a sales relationship with your importer will be covered later in detail.

#7   U.S. Importers Are the Barrier to Entry

This is a curious one to me as an importer, because importers are the way into the U.S. wine market, not the gatekeepers. In my view, and the way in which I have conducted my business for twenty years, importers are the key to business and will open many doors, not just that initial gate to facilitate entry into the U.S. market. And yet, an importer as a "barrier" is exactly the way it was voiced to me not too long ago, and is apparently a common complaint. I imagine it comes from a loose perception of the market as being rigidly preserved for the express and profitable benefit of the wholesaler (importer and distributor are both in that category) when how much easier it would be to be able to sell directly to the restaurant, retail store or even the consumer. Importers are a cog in the wheel of this government imposed system and we must maintain our place in it until the system is overhauled or discarded. Meanwhile, knowledgeable, experienced importers are eminently qualified to assist the foreign producer with entry and sales, and even with a far greater range of distribution than they could normally achieve on their own.

#8   Alcohol and Tobacco Tax and Trade Bureau Can Refuse Entry Based on the Quality of the Wine

The Alcohol and Tobacco Tax and Trade Bureau (TTB) regulates the content of the labels affixed to bottles of alcohol entering this country. They also license importers, exporters and wholesalers and are involved in a number of other regulatory pursuits. But this misconception apparently stems from the erroneous idea that a winery must submit all wine samples to TTB and, on the basis of some undefined and apparently arbitrary level of 'quality', may be refused entry and barred from distribution. This is absolutely not true. Although TTB does require the submission of all wine *labels* to it for approval under rigid guidelines and can, under unusual circumstances, request wine for lab analysis, it is not true that it can or would refuse entry to any brand or any wine based on a perception of quality. If that were the case, many wines already in distribution in this country would never have made it past TTB.

#9 **If a Producer Attends a Trade Tasting Event They Will Meet Many Active and Interested Importers**
Wineries representatives, at considerable expense, travel to the U.S. to attend trade shows put on by various entities, both government sponsored and privately held. These events can be very useful, depending upon many factors such as venue, invitees, preparation by the producer and expectations. They will be a complete waste of time if there is little or no pre-planning, there are no contacts made with interested parties and no appointments made ahead of time. Cost, of both the show itself and other expenses, such as travel and wine, must be factored in to the equation.

#10 **The More Emails Sent and LinkedIn Posts Generated, the Greater the Chance of Finding an Importer**
This is not one of those situations where you play the odds, hoping for a certain percentage return on your general marketing campaign. There are so many emails received by all importers and distributors from wineries seeking representation that generic emails touting the qualities of another unknown brand are going to be deleted. Relationship building is an integral component of the wine business at every stage and just as important at the beginning as it is at any other. We will explore this further in future chapters.

I often see capitalized discussions begun in LinkedIn groups starting with something like WINERY SEEKING IMPORTER. This scattershot approach will rarely, if ever, produce results. Most people who see this type of post will think that the winery is either naive and does not understand even the rudimentary elements of the U.S. market or is desperate because they've exhausted other avenues. A producer seeking representation in the U.S. must find a way to appeal to a potential importer by differentiating their wine from everyone else's, letting the importer know why this will sell for them, and finding the best importer for their individual scenario. LinkedIn is a very useful tool and a valuable resource. However, homework and a focused message will produce much better results.

Current Influences on the U.S. Wine Industry

Much has altered since the economic crash of 2008. Having an inside feel for the changes in the wine industry will help inform any foreign supplier as to whether this is the time to focus on the U.S. market, and what is going to increase the likelihood of success. Changes include:

- Decrease in price paid for wines overall

    Post-2008, many importers found themselves with high priced wines that were no longer affordable and had to slash prices. This led to dumping on the market, importers who went out of business and, in some cases, pushback against certain categories that were associated with expensive wines.

- Expectation of greater value for quality

    With a steady supply of better wines at lower prices, consumers had an opportunity to try wines of higher quality, develop their palates and continue to demand greater value as their disposable income was shrinking. There has also been a trend throughout the world to elevate winemaking technique, vineyard management and overall quality of wines, with a view to creating a competitive edge in a struggling economy, and a growing wine surplus.

- Explosion of social media, affecting buying decisions

    As Twitter, Facebook, blogs and other ways of communicating online exploded, "word-of-mouth" on the Internet has had a key buying

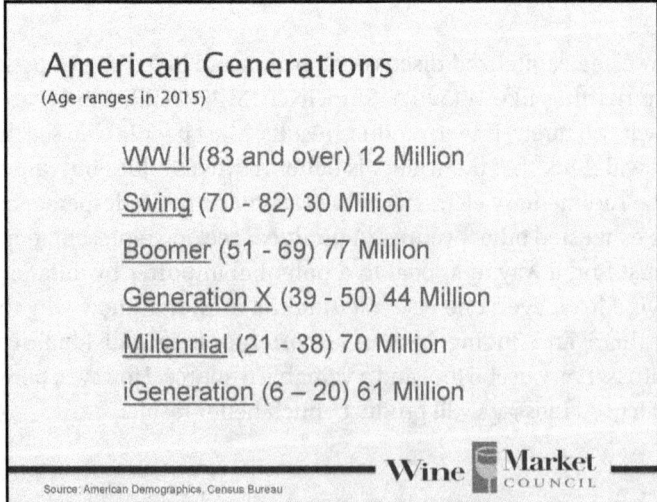

American Generations
(Age ranges in 2015)

WWII (83 and over) 12 Million
Swing (70 - 82) 30 Million
Boomer (51 - 69) 77 Million
Generation X (39 - 50) 44 Million
Millennial (21 - 38) 70 Million
iGeneration (6 – 20) 61 Million

Source: American Demographics, Census Bureau

Wine Market Council

impact. Whether it's finding bargains on a blog that reviews and recommends wines "under $20", for example, or searching for the best online or in-store prices for a certain wine, at any price point, this is the new normal.

- Lesser influence of former rating czars

    Tied to the social media phenomenon in wine buying decisions is the waning influence of the two or three guiding wine raters who could formerly make or break a brand with a number. There are still benefits to reviews and ratings in the main publications, but their influence has been considerably diluted, and in the case of every day or value wines, there are often much more reliable sources. Sophistication, evolution of the rating system and necessity born of the economic downturn have resulted in an altered wine world.

- Rising influence of "Millennials" as consumers

    This group of newly minted wine drinkers has come of legal drinking age in a social media dominated world and many of their own wine buying decisions are predicated on the economic reality they inherited. They expect value, they are adventurous, they don't want to be tied to any preconceptions of an established industry and they're eager to learn more about wine than preceding American generations were at their age.

- Shift in preferred origins and styles

    Partly as a result of natural evolution, what were once emerging trends are now considered mainstream, some newer regions have

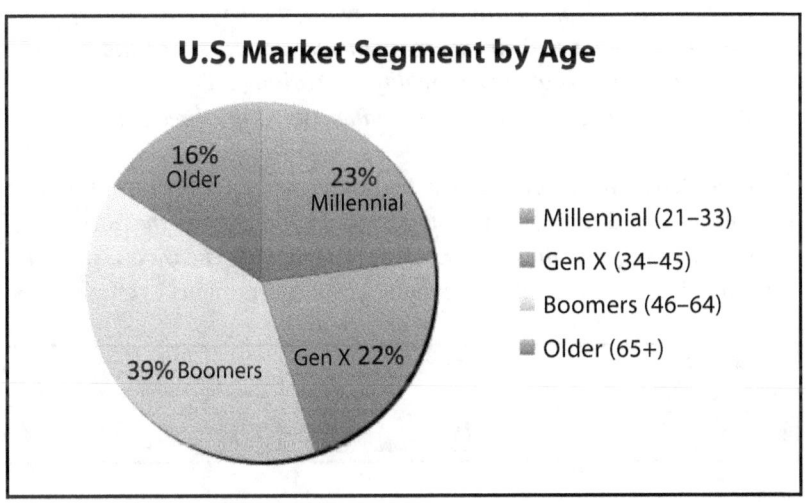

developed to the extent that they can now export, and some of the older, more established regions are falling out of favor. This is one of the most important elements in understanding the U.S. wine industry. Being able to see where your wines fit within current and future trends is paramount to understanding potential, price points, marketability and demand.

An Overview of the U.S. Wine Industry

First and foremost, it is important to understand that this is a heavily regulated wine country. There are fifty different states in the United States. All of them behave as if they are fifty different countries, due in large part to the attitudes and motivations of each state's legislature in the years following Prohibition.

The passage of the 21st Amendment, which repealed Prohibition, resulted in laws that were designed to maintain control over the sale and distribution of alcoholic beverages by different factions, each within their own state's borders, resulting in what is known as the "three-tier system". The three tiers are producers, distributors, and retailers. The basic structure of the system is that producers can sell their products only to wholesale distributors who then sell to retailers, and only retailers may sell to consumers. Producers include brewers, wine makers, distillers and importers.

From Wikipedia:

The only state with a privately operated retailing and distribution system that does not require any form of three-tier system is the State of Washington. In Washington, retailers may purchase alcoholic beverages directly from producers, may negotiate volume discounts, and may warehouse their inventory themselves. However, the three-tier system remains a de facto reality in Washington despite the law. In most situations, the law requires adherence to the three-tier model.

When Pennsylvania created the Pennsylvania Liquor Control Board in 1933, then-Gov. Gifford Pinchot said it would *"discourage the purchase of alcoholic beverages by making it as inconvenient and expensive as possible."* This archaic model for selling alcoholic beverages remains in effect today.

Despite many challenges from wineries and others interested in broadening wine sales, particularly in direct shipping to consumers, the three-tier system has remained relatively unassailable. This is largely due to the vigorous efforts of the Wine and Spirits Wholesalers of America, a trade and lobby organization with many wholesaler members whose interests are served by preserving the status quo.

The three-tier model is true no matter what the circumstances, but often affects spirits and brewers to a greater or lesser degree. As if this wasn't confusing enough, it can be diluted or multiplied in a business model in different circumstances. For example:

- In Control states (discussed later), this model becomes more of a two-tier system, in that the State is both wholesaler and retailer. (Although again there are variations on this, depending upon the state.) Having said that, the three tiers remain in place in theory, since the markups and margins enjoyed by a Control state are similar to those in other states.

- National wholesale distributor chains may appear to circumvent the laws of individual states, when in fact they are adhering to it by establishing (or buying) brick and mortar businesses in each state in which they do business, and operating as licensed entities within the framework of that state's three-tier system.

- A distributor may choose to import one or more of their products for several reasons, such as to have more control over a brand in their portfolio, to realize a double margin on a sale, (i.e. importer and distributor), or even because the distributor was approached by a winery to import their wines exclusively in that region. Normally, their distribution business takes precedence over the importing aspect because they choose to limit their importing to their local area. In this case, it will be understood up front with the winery that there is limited sales potential for their wine, to the extent of the limitations of the individual distribution area.

- An importer can choose to distribute their own products in their state, (the opposite of the above example) by applying for the correct licenses and establishing an office, warehouse and distribution system—the sales and delivery mechanism—and paying the appropriate taxes. Generally, an importer will choose to distribute for some of the same reasons as the wholesaler, but the focus will be the inverse of the wholesaler who chooses to import, because national or regional distribution will require the greater attention. If they have agreed to take on and import a brand for national distribution, expectations would likely be higher that they would be making inroads into multiple states.

In California, for example, an importer can be all parts of the three-tier system and more. An importer may be a distributor and also an online retailer, effectively operating over all three tiers. California wineries have even more latitude in the three areas of wine sales than other licensed entities because of the importance of the wine industry to the California economy. Generally, the line between wholesale and retail in most states is much more restricted.

Tied-House laws are the basis for the three-tier system and relate back to England where laws were put into effect to regulate the sales of alcoholic beverages in bars, pubs and taverns, where the ownership of the entity was "tied" to a specific supplier of alcoholic beverages, who was given an unfair advantage in selling their own products.

According to California Alcoholic Beverage Control (ABC):

Tied house refers to a practice in this country prior to Prohibition and still occurring in England today where a bar or public house, from whence comes the "house" of tied house, is tied to the products of a particular manufacturer, either because the manufacturer owns the house, or the house is contractually obligated to carry only a particular manufacturer's products. The original policy rationale for this body of law was to: 1) promote the state's interest in an orderly market; 2) prohibit the vertical integration and dominance by a single producer in the marketplace; 3) prohibit commercial bribery and protect the public from predatory marketing practices; and, 4) discourage and/or prevent the intemperate use of alcoholic beverages. Generally, other than exceptions granted by the Legislature, the holder of one type of license is not permitted to do business as another type of licensee within the "three-tier" system.

This is no longer true. There have been numerous challenges to the Tied-House laws and successful erosion or evolution has taken place around the country. Much of the opposition comes from large retail chains such as Costco. There will no doubt be more to come as the climate of the wine industry, the business models and the available technology continue to evolve at rapid rates. In any case, you will be relying on your importer, whose job it is to be aware of the most current legal requirements.

Political influence from liquor distributors played a large part in establishing restrictive laws through heavy lobbying efforts that also shape legislation today, spawning and maintaining the three-tier system, which ensures that the distribution of alcohol is regulated separately by each state, in accordance with each state's wishes. It is within this framework that all licensed wine entities—importer, distributor, retailer—must operate today, with the exception of the government controlled states, where the government is both wholesaler and retailer. It was not easy then, and despite some recent erosion of the strictest of laws, it has not become markedly easier today. Those powerful lobbying factions safeguard the status quo, and hamper cross-border wine sales. This is an important consideration for a foreign supplier, as it fundamentally impacts your importer's ability to conduct business, and to what degree, where and how.

Even today, there are some counties within states that maintain Prohibition type laws, remaining "dry" counties, where selling alcohol is illegal.

Fifty Different States—A Potpourri of Cultures

The United States is not just divided by legal borders and state legislatures, but by styles and tastes that characterize diverse regions. These have evolved by immigrant settlement, proximity to each continent (i.e. Europe to East Coast vs. West Coast to Southern Hemisphere), the climate and their local wine production culture. This is another significant consideration when a brand owner begins looking at exporting to the U.S. In the Midwest, for example, there is a large concentration of Germans and Eastern Europeans. In Minnesota (where the ancestry is 29% German), Wisconsin, Illinois, Missouri and Ohio, the extent of German immigration heavily influenced food and therefore wine drinking habits. This is still true today, despite considerable evolution through the generations.

In other states, including those in the Midwest, there is a high proportion of Eastern Europeans, which would leave them open to wines from the Czech Republic, Republic of Georgia, Rumania, etc.

Sweeter wines of various origins are especially popular in the South, due not as much to migration but to acquired tastes. In California, and much of the West, tastes run to New World wines that mirror the styles that California, with its abundant sunshine, produces.

There is always fluidity in any situation, of course, but seeking importers within regions of population concentration that would be receptive to the wines you produce can certainly help the sales of your wines. Having this knowledge before you research appropriate importer matches can help guide both your decision-making and your new importer's efforts.

* * *

Final Thoughts

I am not originally from the United States either. I came here as an adult and began my wine importing company with absolutely no experience. I spent far too long trying to learn the ins and outs of this business on my own, making many expensive mistakes along the way. I not only had to understand the laws and structure, but also the *cultural* distinctions of my adopted country that make the difference in establishing credibility and developing relationships. Debunking myths and shedding light on this confusing market is one step forward in your journey towards finding a home for your wines in the U.S.

2

Breaking Down the States

This is an overview of terminology and practices that you may encounter, not an in-depth breakdown of state laws and regulations. They are simply too complex and disparate to make a study of here, and they are the responsibility of your importer. However, by shedding light on a few similarities through grouping them by statistics, laws, facts and figures, it might be easier for you to understand why choices are made, and why states that seem more desirable may not necessarily be the early focus.

Top Ten Wine States by Volume

1. California   18.1%
2. Florida   8.2%
3. New York   8.0%
4. New Jersey   4.5%
5. Texas   4.5%
6. Illinois   4.5%
7. Massachusetts 3.9%
8. Washington   3.1%
9. Virginia   2.9%
10. Ohio   2.8%

Just these ten states account for 60.5% of total U.S. wine sales. They are considered the top states in which to pursue distribution, also making them the most competitive. More brands are vying for attention, with less room in distributor's inventory and on store shelves. It does not mean there is no opportunity for your wine, but ignoring other opportunities in favor of these states you think you "must" be in, isn't necessarily a sound strategy.

Per Capita Consumption

If you were to look at total alcohol consumption, according to statistics provided by the National Institute on Alcohol Abuse and Alcoholism (NIAAA), the top five states would be:

1. New Hampshire
2. Dist. of Columbia
3. Delaware
4. North Dakota
5. Nevada

These are certainly not the most populous states and would not necessarily be the first states targeted by your importer. However, this is just one illustration to show that you cannot discount the opportunity any state presents, depending upon the circumstances.

Alcoholic Beverage Control and Franchise States

Following the repeal of Prohibition (that archaic and disastrous experiment from 1920-1933 where the sale and consumption of alcohol was outlawed), the 21st Amendment to the Constitution provided states with broad powers and authority to regulate the sale and distribution of alcohol within their borders, resulting in the fifty different sets of laws and regulations in the U.S. today.

Eighteen of those states (which includes only one county in Maryland) continued their own prohibition against anyone else producing, selling or distributing alcohol and by "controlling" the sale of wholesale alcohol. These are known as Control States.

Fourteen of them also control retail sales, which means their citizens purchase liquor at a state package store or designated agency outlet.

Over the decades since the repeal of Prohibition there have been challenges to the laws which have relaxed control or provided the opportunity for free enterprise in certain aspects, such as allowing restaurants to sell wine, or franchising retail stores to individuals. In the case of Maryland, only one county is Control. The rest of the state adopted private licensing.

Control States

Alabama	Idaho	Iowa
Maine	Maryland	Michigan
Mississippi	Montana	New Hampshire
North Carolina	Ohio	Oregon
Pennsylvania	Utah	Vermont
Virginia	West Virginia	Wyoming

Although many of the Control states enable private distribution and sale of wines to some degree and selling to them is not overly onerous, there are some where it is particularly restrictive and where your importer will have different challenges to achieving distribution. The two most restrictive, with the highest government intervention in all sales of alcohol, would be Pennsylvania and Utah. In other states, such as Idaho, Montana and Wyoming, a broker who is familiar with the state system can be very helpful in facilitating sales on your importer's behalf.

Franchise States

Although Control states can impose considerable restriction on alcohol commerce, my opinion is that dealing with Franchise states is fraught with greater jeopardy. This definition, in relationship to the wine industry, refers to the inexplicable and over-reaching protection afforded wholesalers in certain states. It has nothing to do with the concept of franchise as most of us know it. It does not mean assigning rights to an entity to sell recognized goods and services in a cookie cutter format, such as McDonalds or Starbucks. It creates an imbalance in the supplier and wholesaler relationship in a franchise state with considerable partiality to the wholesaler. Although laws vary in each franchise state, essentially it does not permit you to change distributors, even if you want to, even if the wholesaler has not paid its bills, ordered sufficiently from you to make doing business with them worthwhile, or given rise to other non-performance issues.

Franchise laws vary from state to state, with an enormous burden on suppliers in Georgia, for example, and much more relaxed requirements in other states. It is incumbent upon your importer to carefully select and thoroughly vet any selections they make in franchise states.

Currently there are challenges to the laws in several states, which are considered outmoded and unfair. According to the National Association of Wine Retailers:

> *NAWR opposes franchise agreements because despite what conditions they once were meant to address, today they merely serve to provide added anti-competitive protection to wholesalers who have usually purchased this protection through the political power derived from campaign contributions they have gained by being government mandated middlemen. There is no reason to give wholesalers more power than that. The hope is that in Missouri, where the current battle over the Franchise Law is being played out, this dubious notion that wholesalers need added protection from competition will be dismissed both by the state's wine retailers as well as its lawmakers.*

States Ranking for Consumers

According to a comprehensive report by the American Wine Consumer Coalition, the Top 10 Friendliest States for consumers wine laws are:

1. California
2. District of Columbia
3. Missouri
4. Nebraska

5. New Hampshire
6. Oregon
7. Virginia
8. Louisiana
9. Nevada
10. Alaska and Wyoming (Tied for 10th)

This does not necessarily correlate with the distribution for your wine or any other supplier's wines, but overall these are indicators of states whose laws are more conducive to allowing easier legal access to wine.

The same report defines the Top 10 Least Friendly States for consumers:

1. Indiana
2. South Dakota
3. Massachusetts
4. Rhode Island
5. Delaware
6. Kentucky
7. Pennsylvania
8. Mississippi
9. Oklahoma
10. Utah

In this case you can see a correlation between "least friendly" and some of the Control states. Other issues that were taken into consideration were access to wine on Sundays, in restaurants, if BYOB (bring your own bottle) was allowed and so on. One factor worth noting is the following:

States That Ban Wine Sales in Grocery Stores

Alaska	*Massachusetts*	*New York*
Colorado	*Maryland*	*Oklahoma*
Connecticut	*Minnesota*	*Pennsylvania*
Delaware	*Mississippi*	*Rhode Island*
Kansas	*North Dakota*	*Tennessee*
Kentucky	*New Jersey*	*Utah*

Laws change all the time. Your importer, or the wholesaler he or she sells to in that state will be familiar with them, but if, for example, your focus is grocery stores, it is handy to have a reference when considering markets.

* * *

Final Thoughts

With distribution at various times in most states, I have had experience with many different types of state laws. By far the most challenging were the franchise states, and Georgia in particular. There was one wholesaler who took full advantage of state laws by refusing to release my brands, even thought they had not ordered in several months and sales had been declining for a year. I appealed to the State, but they said there were only two alternatives:

1. Stay out of the state for two years
2. Submit detailed reasons with proof for wanting to terminate the agreement with the wholesaler

For me, distribution had been well established and the first option was no option. So I petitioned the state, with a request for a hearing. Since I was required to send a copy of my letter to the wholesaler, it gave them an opportunity to object, which the principal did. He also called and harassed me. It was a harrowing experience for many weeks, until finally the wholesaler relented and granted me the release without further need for a hearing.

Most of my experiences with wholesaler releases in franchise states have been positive, but Georgia wholesalers have enjoyed such protections that it is not at all uncommon for even the most well regarded to require that your newly appointed distributor pick up the wine and pay for it, irrespective of the way it has been stored, or swap a brand from the new wholesaler's portfolio. All reasons for your importer to go into each state fully informed and well prepared.

3

U.S. Importing Alternatives

Some of the options in this chapter address the legal structure options for a U.S. wine importing business. One or more of them may not be open to you, because you are not in a financial, legal or logistical position to take advantage of them, but I mention them so that you are fully apprised of the different ways that an export wine can end up in distribution in the U.S.

Setting up Your Own Import Company

The Alcohol and Tobacco Tax and Trade Bureau (TTB) (www.ttb.gov) is the licensing body for wine, beer and distilled spirits importers in the United States. They are a federal government agency that issues the importing license, called an Importer's Basic Permit. One of the requirements of this license is that the licensee must be a U.S. resident and the licensed place of business must be on U.S. soil. In most instances, the small foreign supplier has no relationship to the U.S., knows no one here who holds an Importer's Basic Permit and is looking for a customer (importer) to simply buy and distribute their wine. However, you may have lived in the States and established relationships through which you have access to someone who could become a viable partner. Or there may be an American who desires to import from a particular region who creates a partnership formed through a relationship developed with someone from that region.

And quite often it is an option for a large or well-funded winery to hire someone in the U.S. as their representative, wholly employed by the winery but established as their importer on the ground. This way, the exporter controls the distribution of their products, has exclusivity in a portfolio and absorbs one of the profit margins in the U.S. (that of importer), in a potentially more lucrative business model. They also control pricing and every other aspect of their U.S. based business. This is more feasible when the exporting winery has both sufficient capital and sales potential to make the investment in an office and employee worthwhile. Setting up your own import company in the U.S. has pros and cons like any other.

Pros

- Control over the process, including investment costs and where business is located
- Control over who runs the import arm and how it is run
- Control over pricing, both at import level and to some extent at retail
- Control over the form this business will take, such as whether to distribute the wines locally, which states to sell to, which wines
- Exclusivity of product, allowing for complete focus on US distribution
- Autonomous decisions regarding launching new wines, vintages, allocations and flow of wines
- Immediate access to sales data and responses to market information

Cons

- Considerable up-front investment in business before wines are sold
- All financial responsibility rests with exporting winery
- Steep learning curve—less likely to have experienced and knowledgeable importer as startup employee
- Lengthy time prior to beginning business while licenses are obtained and business is established
- Lack of control at a distance—meaning that although it is the winery's business investment, some decisions made on the ground in the U.S. can sometimes run counter to the brand owner's desires

- Mistakes can be costly, such as over-supply of wines that are not in demand, high warehousing costs or pricing errors, and become 100% the responsibility of the brand owner
- Reduced maneuverability and loss of time if business model is not working or U.S. employee is not maximizing sales potential

Selling To An Independent Importer

This would be considered the traditional route whereby the exporting winery seeks a U.S. importer already importing other wines and where the new wines would fit within an existing portfolio. Alternatively, a new importer putting together a portfolio for the first time may be a desirable option for your objectives, as long as you understand the advantages and drawbacks to a new venture. Appointing an importer in the U.S. is an option for any brand, from very small production to large scale, but selecting and attracting the most appropriate importer will be discussed in more depth later. For now, we will look at the following considerations.

Pros

- No upfront investment in setting up a business
- Licenses already in place—can get started much faster
- Someone with an established U.S. import business has experience and connections
- Avenues for distribution available earlier because importer already doing business with same wholesalers
- Quick response to market conditions, because importers' investment is at stake
- Payment is made to brand owner for wine in an actual sale
- Investment in ongoing marketing is limited to the brand owner's budget and discretion

Cons

- Most, if not all, decisions regarding sales and marketing of brand owner's wines are now in the hands of U.S. importer
- Wines may not be marketed appropriately or sufficiently to realize potential

- Wines are chosen by importer based on their preference and do not necessarily include your preferences for export
- Sales quantities will be limited to importer's budget, focus, distribution pipeline, personality and perceived potential
- Ongoing orders at the discretion of importer and may not fit with supplier's own needs
- Insufficient notice of new vintages, new orders, marketing timetables
- Lack of communication on aspects of sales that are important to supplier, but for which the importer may not find the time

Setting up a Hybrid Supplier-Importer Business

On the surface, this would appear to combine the best of both worlds and have the greatest potential for sustained success, but it is a much more difficult option to implement. It also requires the most research, travel and meetings with prospective candidates and a fair grasp of the U.S. market. The wines' appeal would have to transcend perceptions of a new, unknown brand to inspire an importer to consider this arrangement.

The ideal scenario would be to involve an established importer in the U.S., with significant distribution channels and who is sufficiently motivated to want to invest in the supplier's brand, aggressively focus on sales and marketing and commit money and personnel with a high likelihood of achieving volume goals. There are several historical examples of this type of relationship; the most famous (in the U.S.) is that between W.J. Deutsch and Yellow Tail, an Australian brand that became the number one imported wine into the U.S., surpassing all French wines combined. The Casella family, owners of Yellow Tail, reached this pinnacle through a combination of factors including savvy marketing, eye-catching label, stylistic appeal and hitting the market at exactly the right time with a value brand. This story has already been told endless times in similar detail in a number of publications and on Yellow Tail's own website. Although much has been made of the synchronicity of events and decisions, in my opinion as an importer, what really catapulted them to the front of the line in the U.S. was the decision to collaborate with W. J. Deutsch to import and market their wines in a 50/50 partnership. This financial investment and the probability of significant profits is what motivated W.J. Deutsch to ensure that the brand was represented in their distribution network throughout the country and remains the quintessential example of the ideal supplier/importer collaboration.

Despite this, Yellow Tail encountered difficulties maintaining margin and position as the weak U.S. dollar eroded their profits and their own model constrains price increases. (They have recently expanded the line in response to market conditions, which is likely to bolster the brand's future.) To duplicate their level of sales success with a partnership would not be easy under the present economic conditions, but there may be other importers and other brands with just the right combination of attributes to make it happen. A more likely scenario is a partnership that allows for shared responsibility and a reasonable degree of profitability for both parties. The possible pros and cons to this are as follows.

Pros

- Both invested in the outcome
- Shared financial investment
- Shared accountability
- A U.S. partner who will work hard to achieve desired results
- Equal partners in decision-making
- Ability to capitalize on individual strengths of each partner off-shore and in the U.S.
- The opportunity for faster and larger growth

Cons

- More demands made on the supplier to create wines for U.S. importer's market model
- Potential brand identity changes that run contrary to supplier's image
- Greater demands made on supplier's resources and time
- A new importer who may not have the necessary connections and distribution channels
- In the event that one of the two parties wants to opt out of the relationship the merged business may be difficult to separate, sell or transition to someone else

Appointing a Compliance Importer

I mention this one to complete a comprehensive look at this subject and for you to understand the nuances of various options, but I'm not advocating it, unless you can meet at least one of these criteria:

1. You have access to distribution or demand for sales that you cannot fill because you do not have a traditional importer
2. You will be making numerous trips to work the markets yourself, or plan on living here part-time
3. You have a trusted representative on the ground in the U.S. who can sell product in areas of distribution provided by the compliance company

What I am calling a 'compliance' importer is not an actual name for this type of importer. Wine importer means only one thing in the wine industry and to TTB, but I use it as a term to differentiate it from a 'traditional' importer model. It is a perfectly legitimate enterprise, licensed according to alcoholic beverage laws and holding a Federal Basic Permit entitling them to import wines. This type of entity usually services the needs of U.S. companies who wish to relinquish control of their compliance (i.e. licenses, brand registrations, monthly reporting and all that is involved in federal and state regulatory guidelines) and who will also be able to take advantage of licenses in their home state, and possibly warehousing options. It is important to note that this type of company is not designed to find distribution for you, nor can they assist in sales. If you simply see it as a way to get your product onto U.S. soil, I advise against it. There is no way to truly monitor your wines and a high degree of probability that they will sit in a warehouse accumulating fees, selling slowly or not at all.

* * *

Final Thoughts

When I first started my import business, my father, who had connections in the wine industry in Australia, was instrumental in putting together a consortium of very small, limited production Australian brands with no export experience and no connections of their own to retain me as their U.S. importer. This was actually a hybrid of some of the models I have outlined in this chapter, in that I retained my independence as a single entity importer, but my obligation was solely to these suppliers. Each of them paid a monthly stipend, which allowed me to establish my business and allowed them to export with some assurance that they had a trustworthy importer at this end. It had advantages and disadvantages, not the least of which was that although none of us on either end had any experience, these were very small wineries with obscure wines, with no other way (at that time) to gain access to an importer. For a fairly small investment they had an opportunity to secure sales in the U.S. It certainly was the catalyst for business expansion for me, and was a modestly successful venture overall. Brands that were priced appropriately, suited the American palate and had attractive packaging did well; those that lacked these attributes were unable to gain a foothold and fell away. I believe this would have happened irrespective of who was handling their brands. Perhaps my success was more modest than some, but certain brands would not even have had the necessary qualities to retain an importer in the first place. It was our collective naiveté that provided the catalyst for an exploratory venture.

Exporting is achievable through different avenues, depending upon which structure you are able to put in place, have access to, or appeals to you as having the greatest likelihood of success, as long as you remember to comply with U.S. regulations in any model.

A Role Defined

When considering the traditional model—finding and appointing an importer—we should first explore what an importer does and how.

Importer as Gatekeeper

A properly licensed wine importer holds an Importer's Basic Permit, a federal license issued by the Alcohol and Tobacco Tax and Trade Bureau (TTB). Obtaining a license entails a comprehensive application, background information (and sometimes a background check), an inquiry into the source of funds for their business, references, determination that they are a legal U.S. resident and a phone interview. A "letter of intent" from an export winery must be attached to the application stating that they intend to supply the importer with their alcoholic product (only one is required in the beginning, not one for each winery at every stage).

The Importer's Basic Permit allows the licensee to import wine into the U.S., sometimes exclusively and at other times as one of several importers throughout the country for the same products, but in different territories, per agreement with the foreign supplier. Irrespective of whether they are exclusive or one of many, an importer is the only person, or licensed company, to which you may sell wines. This is an important concept to remember. There is no other alternative to importing wine into the U.S. for the purpose of resale. There are creative ways to establish sales, promote your wines and market and grow your business, but they all must pass through an importer's license to be legal.

An importer can be located in any state in the country, as long as they also hold appropriate licenses in their home state. These would include a license to warehouse and to import into that particular state, and others according to the state. *Import*, in this case, refers to the state requirements, which are separate and apart from the federal import regulations. The importer must also adhere to requirements outside their home state in any state in which they plan to sell their wines to wholesalers for distribution. This can vary from brand registration, licensing, label approvals, contracts and permits.

It becomes evident that it is a heavily regulated process and why the professional on the ground must be familiar with all requirements and follow strict protocol when it comes to alcohol distribution in the U.S.

An importer may sell to distributors in all fifty states, or decide to limit sales to their home state, or a narrowly prescribed geographical area (such as counties within the state), or a limited collection of states with contiguous borders. The latter examples may be because the importer is confident that they can manage and maintain sales in a smaller, more focused way. They also have more control over their distribution, especially in their home state where, in addition to the importer license, they may also become licensed as distributor of the wines they import. The value in this to you, the supplier, is the immediate access to a distribution network. However, if you want to grow the brand into other states, it will be necessary to find and appoint other importers.

Your appointed importer will secure compliant label approvals for the brands they represent and, in addition to initial licensing requirements, ongoing reporting and license renewals are maintained so that continuity is ensured for your brand.

A savvy, experienced importer can advise you on packaging, pricing and style advantages. This does not mean ignoring your own aesthetics or your brand identity, but if it is evident that a label will not work in this market, either because it does not clearly define expectations for the wine or it is confusing and off-putting, then changes must be made.

This is a conversation reported by an importer on LinkedIn about a trade show they had attended, repeated verbatim:

Importer: Your label will not work in the U.S. because it will not stand out.

Producer: Why should I change the label to make it stand out more?

Importer: You have a house on the label.

Producer: And?

Importer: So do the other ten wineries on this row alone.

The point of this conversation, and many others like it, is that the importer who is either experienced or has researched his market sufficiently well, will immediately understand the need to advise the exporter on launching their brand to best advantage. I cannot tell you how many European labels I have seen depicting a nondescript house or vineyard. It may be significant and evocative to you but, as with many personal and subjective parts of our own lives, they will have no meaning for anyone else. If done well, with flair, good taste and creativity, the label could work. But most often they look like many others of any region. What is the point of doing all this work to produce excellent wine and seek out export markets, only to be impeded by your attachment to a label?

Not all labels appeal to everyone, but these are examples of wine labels demonstrating a nod to region and price point.

The brand depicted in Figure 4 utilizes the art of Alfonse Mucha, a Czech Art Nouveau painter with each label depicting a different painting. This is positioned as a 'premium' brand. The brand depicted in Figure 5 depicts the gaucho, the nationalistic symbol in Argentina in a fun, 'popular' price range. The brand depicted in Figure 6 is closely tied to the name itself and has achieved a following for the combination of name, image and age of the wine.

Nor should your pricing decisions be arbitrary. Unlike someone who wants to merely cut prices so that they can have an easier time selling a high quality wine for much less, a good importer has logical reasons why the winery price needs to be adjusted down, either from analyzing the market or from their own experience with competitive wines.

The importer role also involves familiarity with freight forwarders, weighing options for ocean freight companies and payment of duties and taxes to clear customs. Capably and economically handling logistics once the wine reaches port in the U.S., such as transporting containers to the warehouse, maintaining inventory and overseeing sales channels and volume throughout the country are also part of their responsibilities.

A gatekeeper they may be, but it is not with the intent to limit access to a supplier partner, but to operate within the guidelines that the U.S. government has laid out to license and regulate alcohol distribution.

32 THE EXPORTER'S HANDBOOK TO THE US WINE MARKET

Figure 4 Czech label

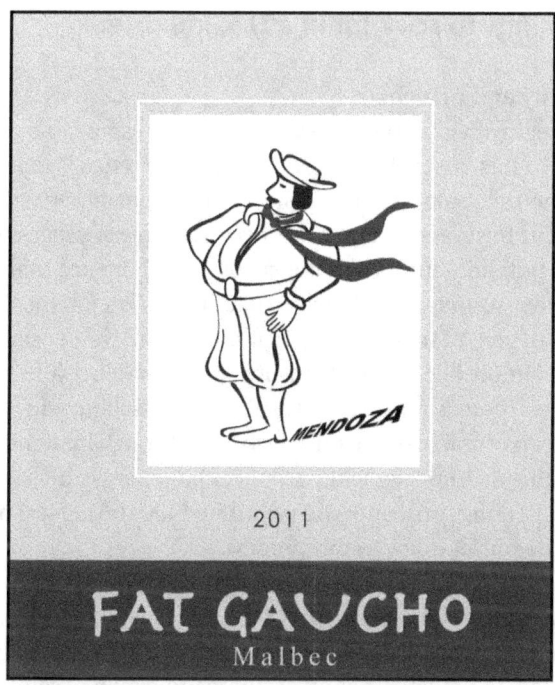

Figure 5 Argentine label

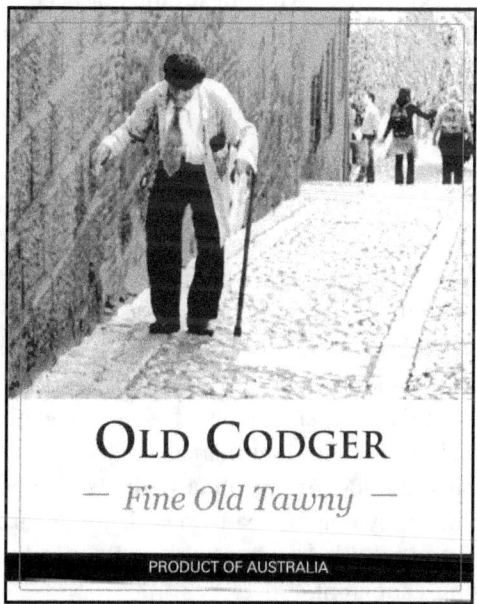

Figure 6 Old Codger label

Top Ten Things to Look for in a U.S. Importer

#1 Integrity and principles

This might seem obvious, but there are as many irresponsible or unscrupulous people in this business as any other. The difference is that you are not making a one-time sale; you are setting up a partnership where integrity is crucial to your business and vital for success. I am not suggesting that you approach a potential importer with suspicion. There are many elements of an importer/supplier relationship that depend on a handshake agreement and a degree of trust to work, but don't be naive in establishing the relationship simply because you are anxious to establish your brand in the United States. There is nothing to be gained from selling wine to someone who does not pay or allows the business to fail through inattention. Finding and appointing an importer takes a lot of effort, energy and some financial investment. Finding someone who pays their bills and at least has the right attitude at the outset is key to this process.

#2 A Clear Vision for Your Brand

This does not necessarily mean that the importer knows exactly what they want to do with your wines, has an accurate projection of sales, where they will be distributed and how. That requires a crystal ball at the outset, where there is no historical context. What it calls for, however, is someone who has an understanding of the wine styles and origin, where they fit in the market, how they should be marketed and a desire to implement a strategy to launch and develop your brand.

#3 The Right Fit for Them

If the importer only imports from Argentina and your wines are from Bulgaria, will this importer be willing to switch gears to develop a market for wines from a fairly unknown Eastern European region? Or will they be floundering with these more austere wines amid their New World full-bodied portfolio? This does not necessarily mean they cannot make this adjustment or take their portfolio in a new direction, but there has to be a reason to do so and an understanding of where the wines you represent will fit within their vision and their market. They could conceivably have exhausted their distribution for Argentina, or they see a decline in sales for a saturated region. They may be ready to seek out lesser known regions with more opportunity. This is a discussion to have with the importer so that the fit becomes apparent.

#4   The Right Fit for You

This may seem like a duplicate category, but I am referring more to the personality fit between the supplier and the importer. This is a partnership and, like all partnerships, if there is no common ground, a lack of ability to relate or friction, it will eventually break down. Not all will become evident at the beginning, but considering a "gut check" as one of the criteria allows you to look at the prospective importer through the lens of a relationship, rather than a vendor/buyer transaction.

#5   The Geographical Reach You Need

With this item, "need" becomes subjective, rather than overarching. Considerations that matter to you will also have to dovetail with your importer's desires. Do you have sufficient wine to supply the whole country or only a small area? Are your wines exclusive and expensive and will be limited in demand to a certain demographic? Do you have low-priced high volume wines which have the potential to be distributed throughout the country? Can this the importer achieve that?

#6   Small Enough for Your Wines to be an Important Component, but Large Enough to Provide Reach

This can be a delicate balance, involving consideration of the importer's ability to pay and sustain their business model. A smaller importer is likely to place much more emphasis on your wines, because they have less competition within the portfolio vying for their attention and they need the income the sales will provide. Clearly there should be discussions on how much time they intend to devote to your wines and how much time overall they devote to the rest of the brands they represent. On the other hand, you don't want an importer whose business is so small that this is a part-time hobby, devoting time to wine sales when they're not directing their efforts to their unrelated full-time occupation.

#7   The Ability to Grow with Your Business

An importer should either be a catalyst for your sales growth or poised to capitalize on the growth your wines achieve on their own merits. What are the importer's goals? How far do they want to go? If expansion for your brand is meteoric, there may need to be a discussion on the partnering aspect, because a small importer may not have the funds to support this type of rapid distribution development and the travel, marketing, shipping and logistics budget this would require. A happy circumstance to contemplate!

#8   Not So Large That There is No Focus on Your Products

This really is an important issue because a large importer with an extensive distribution network will seem ideal for anyone, and often they are. But the danger is that they may be initially enthusiastic about your brand and bring in a container, only to find that it competes too heavily with existing wines or they cannot find the time to devote sufficient attention to your brand. Because they are large, they have many successful brands churning out sales and it is easy to discard a brand that isn't working. The decision to bring in your wines could have been part of a plan to expand into different regions, a genuine zeal for the synergy they appear to offer, or a desire to ride a wave of popularity. It could be because the brand was originally with another importer and they thought they could immediately fill a waiting pipeline with product. Whatever the reason, there are just as many ways in which these become unfulfilled dreams. Dialogue at the outset will be valuable to both sides in understanding motivation and objectives.

#9   Financial Stability

In an effort to secure importation and distribution of your wines in the U.S., the financial stability of a potential—and interested—importer can be swept aside in the excitement. This does not necessarily mean that all importers should be wealthy or have a significant financial cushion, but they should be able to pay for your products and budget for product flow and contingencies. Their historical record and reputation will become evident when you exercise your due diligence and you will have the fundamental tools to make a decision as to what risks you are willing to take.

#10   Flexibility and Objectivity

Will your potential importer be willing to consider your opinions, desires, objectives and plans for your brand? Will you be willing to consider alternatives, based on their experience? Can the potential importer put aside preconceived notions about the varieties or styles of wine from your region and entertain something unusual and unknown? Will you be willing to put aside your own potentially narrow perspective and consider what will or will not work in the U.S.? Not every importer can be a vanguard for change, but making room for the esoteric in the portfolio shows a predisposition to adapt. Welschriesling may not be a familiar wine to many Americans, but Grüner Veltliner is, and having both from a brand, in varying degrees of volume, will demonstrate what the region can produce. The former will require far more dedication and time to sell, but a willingness to import and devote time to introducing small quantities of a somewhat obscure wine could determine the importer's commitment to the brand. This is, of course, predicated on an assumption of the wine's favorable quality and price ratio. No importer should feel compelled to bring in wines that have little chance for success and become an exercise in futility.

Beginning your search for an importer with a list of reasonable requirements will give you a clearer understanding of what you should be looking for, what type of importer meshes with your individual business model and whether there is the potential for a long-term relationship.

How to Find an Importer

As I touched on in the misconceptions section, I see many misguided attempts by foreign wineries to find a U.S. importer. I know their efforts are doomed to failure, but no one has given these wineries an effective way to approach a prospective American business partner. They are eager to succeed, but woefully lacking in any experience or knowledge of this market. Their initial approach lacks focus, stated intent and specificity. And if someone responds, the winery still has no idea if the responder is an appropriate candidate. So, we'll start with some reasons why a brand is not likely to attract an importer during the initial phase:

- Failure to understand how the U.S. market works in any way, resulting in approaching the wrong people (or entertaining approaches from the wrong people)
- Lack of research on states and identifying specific importers
- Lack of focus on which type of importer and to whom your brand might appeal
- Scattershot approach to an unknown and inappropriate list of importers
- Poor grasp of English reflected in email, rendering it incomprehensible (even a Google translation is often preferable)
- Generic email without personalization, or to the wrong person
- Promotional post in LinkedIn that is non-specific and sounds desperate
- Failure to follow up in communication

Who has time to waste churning out emails, whether they are articulately worded, or Google translated, to entities that have no interest? Whether you are a wealthy French château owner with extensive staff or a lone farmer/winemaker with a small brand in New Zealand, your time is best spent on a focused endeavor with a fair likelihood of achieving your goals. I personally receive around twenty emails a week from brand representatives wanting me to consider their wines for my portfolio. I have no interest in bringing in new wines and have never imported wines from Italy or Germany, among other countries. The majority of emails are addressed to me as "Dear Sir" or sometimes as "Dear Sir/Madam" and once even "Dear Fredrik". I recently received one that began, "To the kind attention of the Purchasing Department" and then went on to say, "As you may remember, we have already contacted you...". None of these is likely to impress me, but the latter says they have already made one generic attempt that has produced no result. What suggests to them that this approach will be any different? Not to know whether I am male or female, or indeed *have* a "purchasing department", tells me that there is no attempt to research my suitability for their wines. If they are going to be this indifferent or careless in their initial approach, it does not bode well for future interaction.

Think of this as a resume and cover letter applying for an executive position with a company you really want to work for. Of course you won't be your importer's employee, but many of the same principles apply.

- Know the importer's name
- Demonstrate at least a rudimentary understanding of this market
- Establish an awareness of the importer's area of interest or expertise
- Tailor your approach to their needs
- Indicate how you might provide value to them
- Itemize the strengths of the brand

Why do they need you? What synergy might be established between you and their company? Just like an employer, they want to know that their choice will be an asset to their business. It's a great deal of work and investment on both sides to enter into this type of relationship, so the initial impression is very important.

How specifically can you go about finding an importer so that the approach I outlined above finds the right target? There are a number of different ways and while no one is guaranteed to succeed, they all provide more opportunity than the generic email blast.

Take a look at your brand first. Consider what your market would look like if you represented one of the following.

A High End Brand with Limited Production and Laudatory Press

This starts to suggest an importer with a select number of distributors and a specialized knowledge of more expensive, small production wines, or an importer with top restaurant and hotel connections. They would likely have traveled extensively and have a solid knowledge base about the regions and wines they represent. But what about your own wine origins? Bordeaux is going to be far different from Chile, for instance. The expectations for Bordeaux are high end, specific, elite. Whereas Chile has a reputation for value priced, large volume brands. That is not to say there can't be inexpensive Bordeaux or premium Chilean wines, but perception will mean a lot during the introduction of the wines. Your ideal importer can be many things, but someone who is accustomed to importing and selling wines to high profile distributors and getting into top accounts may be a good choice for this type of brand.

A Range of Wines Across Price Points, Styles and Varietals

It would now depend on the region. Let's take Uruguay as an example. If your wines are from Uruguay, which is relatively unknown to the average American consumer, then perhaps the ideal importer would represent Argentina in their portfolio, as a way to transition from one region sharing borders with another. It will also allow the importer to expand their range into something interesting and unusual, while also expanding their distribution potential. If your brand is from France or Italy, the right fit might be an Italian or French specialist or it could be a portfolio that represents a cross-section of Europe; likewise with the Southern Hemisphere. The key to attracting this type of importer will probably be the degree to which you have familiarized yourself with the U.S. market, your expectations and willingness to commit to being a collaborative marketing partner with your importer. The two companies—supplier and importer—would remain separate, but in this highly competitive market, the importer would want to know they have a supplier who is willing to support their efforts when needed. More on that later.

High Volume, Value Priced, "Over-Delivering" Wines

This might depend on the region of origin and the style. For instance, it is unlikely, at this time, that a similarly priced and sourced brand from Australia could do very well against a powerhouse like Yellow Tail. This is a brand that has virtually cornered the under $10 retail price point for this style in an economic market of value conscious wines. But if your expectations are kept in check, there could be exponential growth over time. The right importer for this type of brand is likely to be someone with broad reach, chain connections and an appreciation of the way to sell higher volume and keep the supply chain moving. They would be energetic, motivated and persistent and have strong relationships in this very competitive field.

In researching importers for all needs, styles and price points, also consider these questions:

- Where are the importers' gaps in either regions or price points? For example, if they have French wines, are they missing Rhône and Loire? If they are an Australian importer, are most of their wines from Barossa Valley or Mudgee?
- What niche could you fill? As an example, is there a different varietal or wine style from a region they already represent that you could provide? Does your brand represent a price point that appears to be lacking in their portfolio?
- How do your wines compare with what the importer already represents? Are the wines comparable, better priced, more accessible styles?
- Do your wines have recognizable accolades that could provide an advantage? (This refers to gold medals or Decanter and other internationally recognized confirmations of quality, not local recognition.)

The tangible ways in which you could go about finding an importer include the following.

Trade Shows and Wine Fairs

Where your focus goes, your energy flows.

It never ceases to amaze me that a foreign winery—and this applies to a wine brand owner from any country—will often willingly splurge on an extravagant wine fair, trade show or tasting event without the slightest understanding of what will happen, who is attending and whether it is a beneficial, or even viable, path to finding an importer. I do empathize. If information to the contrary is not readily available to you, the idea of a wine event on U.S. soil seems like a gateway to interested U.S. importers. Especially if it appears to be well promoted or is endorsed by a government trade agency. But after event fees, wine samples, shipping, customs clearance, air fare, hotel and food costs, the supplier very often returns to their home country with a fistful of business cards and little else. It is a broad brush approach to something that requires focused, careful attention in the planning and equally meticulous follow up.

First of all, let's take the government sponsored event. Trade organizations representing countries or regions can be very helpful in sourcing business, pointing the winery in the right direction or providing tips on the U.S. market, but they can also be much more focused on promoting the *whole country* than the individual winery. Foreign trade organizations on U.S. soil often represent their country's locally produced food as well and their knowledge and experience within the wine industry may be limited. As such, the event may include seafood or specialty foods, be loosely organized around a collective national identity and not necessarily be attracting the right audience. The event may fulfill marketing objectives within the sponsor's annual government-allocated budget, but end up with event goals that conflict with a winery exporter's expectations. On the positive side, they are non-profit and should be relatively affordable and, if the organizers have been listening to their constituency or consulted with experienced marketers with good connections, it could be a well-attended event.

An independent, for-profit wine fair will often be splashier, extensively marketed, well organized, in a desirable location and EXPENSIVE. I've seen one show charge as much as $48,000 for an exhibitor's 'pavilion'. At such an event, a booth is around $3,000. Whether these shows attract the right audience and a range of potential partners for a new exporter's products remains in doubt. There is often a disconnect between the event organizer's objectives and the event attendees. Even less certain is whether the exporter will ever recoup the expense for such a costly event in wine sales.

There are wine events, fairs or even conventions that are exceptionally worthwhile, but it requires investigation and preparation. You cannot assume that if someone in the U.S. is organizing it, they must know what they're doing. You also cannot assume that their goals align with yours.

As a winery interested in coming to the U.S. for the express purpose of finding representation for your wines, the questions to ask yourself, or event planners, are these:

- **When is the event held?** Ideally, it should be on the cusp of seasonal buying times and not directly in competition with high profile events in the same week that will draw trade away.
- **Where is the venue?** How expensive is it? It should be somewhere that attracts attendees, but not so expensive as to make it

prohibitive to both exhibitor and attendee. Most events are free to the trade to attend.

- **Who is invited?** What is the caliber of invitee and level of interest? The organizers should ensure that importers and distributors with interest in adding to their portfolios are the main invitees. These are your customers. Without an importer, your wines cannot be distributed, but often distributors also have an import license. A trade show that relies heavily on retail attendees is only beneficial if you have existing U.S. distribution.

- **Can you get the list of importers and distributors?** Being able to contact them beforehand to let them know you will be exhibiting and where you will be located is the first step in determining interest. Researching their qualifications ahead of the event will also allow you to make some decisions about whether they might be a good fit for your wines.

- **How many wineries are exhibiting?** There should be sufficient number and diversity to make this an attractive event and a draw card for invitees.

- **Are consumers included?** If so, what is the trade/consumer ratio? Sometimes a charitable portion is included, or consumers are invited at higher entrance fees, to help defray event costs for the trade. You must be gracious and pay attention to this segment but this is not your customer and their enjoyment of your wine will not sell it to a wholesale partner. Your *entire objective* must be to find an importer, whether it's someone for one state or fifty. Otherwise, this

Figure 7 New York wine tasting held at the Czech consulate

is a wasted exercise. Anyone *else* who tries your wines, and falls in love with them, will not be able to find them for sale and will forget about them shortly after the event, or at least long before you are able to ship wine and establish distribution.

- **Who is your brand representative?** It is absolutely essential that either you, the winemaker or brand owner attend the event, or you send someone from your company who is going to be knowledgeable about your wines, is able to make decisions, is personable, has a reasonable understanding of the U.S. market and will make the right impression. Additionally, they must be prepared to follow up and follow *through* with their contacts.

Not long ago, I attended a well-organized wine event in New York that exemplifies my point about a focused trade event. It was held at the Czech consulate in a beautiful, high ceilinged space with large windows, Czech crystal chandeliers and old wooden floors, and hosted by the Czech Consul General (see Figure 7). Already this has all the earmarks of an event that is likely to attract the jaded New York wine trade, despite featuring all esoteric and unknown Moravian wines.

Added to that, it was highlighted in *World Trade Week in New York* publicity and the wineries and importer who organized the event were immensely aided by the mailing list of the Czech consulate. It attracted not only a fine wine trade component, but also interested and connected New York elite (see Figure 8).

Figure 8   Wine lineup at Czech consulate tasting

There were other elements that will provide ongoing exposure for the wines:

- A PR firm that signed in the trade and press, gathering contact details for the future
- A photographer who memorialized the event, and provided useful photos for additional marketing
- Recognition of press by the principals that gave them a more knowledgeable tasting experience and resulting blog posts and articles that kept the momentum going

For the organizing importer it was an opportunity to see what could be added to his own portfolio, and for anyone else interested in importing Czech wines, it was an exercise in the appeal these wines might have to the market.

In addition, the organizer partnered with a trade organization in the Czech Republic, which financially contributed to the event with support for samples, shipping and travel expenses. This really was a case study in a successful wine event. Whether it will ultimately result in representation or success for all brands concerned remains to be seen. Quality, appropriate pricing, marketability and follow-up still must play a major role in any endeavor, irrespective of how well the stage has been set.

A wine show is just one way to market. There are many others. However, a brand owner that relies on this venue as their only way to an importer, without doing their homework, is bound to be disappointed.

Foreign Trade Organizations

This avenue can be a little tricky, because there are many well-meaning trade organizations that want to promote the wines of their own locale, either as a government-sponsored effort to foster trade or as a consortium put together by wineries to raise awareness for their particular region, and hopefully find distribution in the process. Many foreign trade organizations will organize events, in addition to engaging in wine promotion efforts through retail marketing, print and online press releases and articles and activities tailored to the needs of their constituency. If it is an organization with a long history in the U.S. such as the Italian Wine and Food Institute, www.italianwineandfoodinstitute.com or the French Trade Commission, www.ubifrance.com (as examples only), both of which are actively involved in focused events and efforts to promote their country's products, this type of agency can be an indispensable resource. Foreign trade organizations embrace a broad spectrum of products, including food, fashion and regionally specific exports. They also organize events expressly around wine and food, with an approach that combines the two harmoniously. I have provided a partial list of trade organizations for many different countries (see page 203). At the very least, they can offer the benefit of their experience and recommendations to other avenues better suited to your particular situation.

I have attended wine events at embassies where raw oysters were being shucked for the pleasure of the guests, locally produced meats were offered for sampling, or where vendors were showcasing their artisanal spreads and cheeses to complement the same region's wines. In addition to the anticipated quality of the wines, this all adds to the overall impression of a country's identity, and usually ensures a higher attendance. Once again, inquire about the type of attendee. Will there be importers, distributors, retailers, restaurateurs? Although your target is an importer, having the other representatives of trade in the mix enables you to gauge reaction to your wines and often creates a sense of buzz around their quality and desirability. Many of these people will know one another. If a sufficient number of attendees are telling others to go and try the wines at your table, it raises the demand quotient and potential for importer interest.

If, for example, you are part of a region where the emerging wineries decide to get together to join forces and hold an event in the U.S. to attract importers, in this case there is no historical record or experience to fall back on. Your region may be a young area where vineyards are just beginning to produce sufficient quantity for export markets. Or it may be an older, but recently organized sub-region that wants to differentiate itself from others. Whatever the impetus, there is every reason to consider such an event, and every reason to decline if all the factors I have mentioned are absent.

As with any expenditure, you will be well advised to consider what your outlay will be and whether it is worth it. With recurring annual events, if you can ask others about their experiences in prior years or their expectations of this year, it will enable you to make a more informed decision as to whether to participate.

Completely aside from the trade show event format, if your country has an active trade organization in the U.S., it can offer valuable perspective on the American market for your particular country and may even have a list of interested or current importers who already import from your country.

Internet Website Search

There is a website called www.bestwineimporters.com that catalogs names (for purchase) of wine importers in various countries around the world. It is an extensive compilation, but from my familiarity with some of the names on it I know, without a doubt, that this is not a list of the best wine importers in the U.S.; it is simply a list, incorporating good, bad and mediocre. In fact, I know of one in particular that has been sued on numerous occasions and it remains a mystery to many of us as to how this importer remains in business. It is a classic example of why you should not trust others to do your research for you, or blindly accept assurances that a particular method of connecting suppliers and importers will be effective.

If you choose to purchase this catalogue or have a collection of contacts from some other source, my caveat is once again: do not take the *easy way out.* No blanket emails to the importers! You do not know any of them yet. This is the same as the generic email blast that will most likely be deleted when it lands in an inbox. Aside from any issue of where and how you derived the list, they may or may not be effective importers; they may or may not be importing anything from your part of the world; they may or may not be in the right category for you, that is, their emphasis may be volume brands to supermarkets or, conversely, small production, family-owned vineyards. So the next step is to take a look at the importer's website. How does it look—dynamic, updated, effective trade tools, etc.? What regions do they represent? Does their portfolio comprise high volume or hand crafted wines? What else does it say about them, such as who they are and their time in business. I have given you below some examples of importer websites that tell a story. These are *not* specific recommendations, although these are all reputable importers, in my opinion. I am not suggesting they are looking for new brands: they are simply an illustration of the information you can mine from a good U.S. importer's website to assist you in your quest.

    www.obcwines.com

    www.eamericanestates.com

    www.weygandtmetzler.com

You will find many others on your own. Perhaps you recognize a winery on a website you have researched. Perhaps a brand from your country, or one you have encountered at wine events. How do you feel about their wines and philosophy? Do they complement your wines? Are they too close in region, style, price point or quite different in these areas? Could you speak to them about their experience with this importer? Whatever information you have gathered from the website that informs your choice of target importers, make sure to personalize your initial approach with an introduction that includes why you are contacting them. The initial contact can be via email or phone, but limit it to a short, succinct contact that immediately captures their attention. No differently from a job application, or 'cold call' selling, you want to let this email recipient know you have done your homework and have a specific reason for reaching out to them. It is part flattery, part appropriate professionalism and part good business sense. Assuming you have targeted someone who is even considering new brands, your approach often translates to a perception on the part of the importer that if you are willing to take the time to identify their characteristics and suitability to import your brand, there is a greater likelihood that you will also be a supportive, collaborative, proficient partner.

Wine Brands—Reverse Importer Search

A type of reverse search for an importer is to consider which wine brands you have high regard for and that seem to be doing well in the States, as opposed to what you recognize from a website. This does not necessarily mean the wines of your neighbors or even your specific region, but in general. Perhaps these are wines you enjoy with dinner, encountered in travel, or that have achieved some prominence in stores; it could be a well-regarded Château or a brand with significant ratings and awards. Perhaps you have no idea if this is a prominent brand or one that sells well in the States, but you start your web search with a name. It doesn't matter what the wine is or how yours compares to it, only that it is one you admire or feel gives a sense of something you want from an importer, whether it be gravitas, sense of place, volume capacity or anything else you have identified as important to you.

In the Internet search bar on your computer, type in "U.S. wine importer (name of brand)". This will bring up a variety of results, depending upon the wine or brand you choose. For the sake of this experiment, let's say you choose Château d'Yquem. So you will type in: "U.S. wine importer Château d'Yquem". Things change fast in the wine industry these days, but at this time it brings up some interesting results that cover a fairly broad spectrum. For instance, the first search result that appeared on the page when I searched was an Arizona distributor, Quail Distributing, www.quaildistributing.com. They are not the importer for d'Yquem, but it was on their site that I found a number of importers, in addition to the U.S. importer for Château d'Yquem. This kind of search would be an excellent place to start exploring, if in fact you are searching for an importer of this category.

The next search result was actually the importer for Château d'Yquem, which, at this time, is Moët Hennessy, www.mhusa.com, quite an exclusive importer with some of the most famous and marketable brands, such as Moët & Chandon (France), Veuve Clicquot (France), Cloudy Bay (New Zealand), Dom Perignon (France), Cape Mentelle (Australia) and more. This may not be at all the type of portfolio appropriate to your wines. I offer it only to illustrate a point. There is naturally a preponderance of French brands among Moët & Chandon's portfolio, but they are not so Eurocentric that they exclude the Southern Hemisphere. To attract an importer like this, it would be very important to have a select brand with unique characteristics in terroir and wines. Or possibly you should just bypass this importer altogether in favor of an organization that would be a better match. Either way, this information gives you valuable context for your search, rather than just a name.

Rounding out the same example, examine Quail Distributing's site further, not as a prospective importer (they are a state wholesaler) but as a resource in your search for prospective importers for your brand. By making this a 'reverse' search, looking for a wine rather than an importer, you may find the type of importer that appears to express your vision for your wines through their choice of representation of other brands.

In the past, when I was seeking distributors for the wines I imported, I would periodically use this method if I had exhausted my own connections in various states. Nothing is foolproof and nothing is achieved without the aforementioned due diligence, but it is a method that proved to work for me on occasion.

Just remember that importers are different from distributors. You are looking for an *importer* first. It is their job to appoint distributors in other states, unless you decide that you wish to find and negotiate with a different importer in each of the fifty states to distribute your brand within their own distribution region. Having several different importers in the U.S. may be a personal preference, or may present itself based on interest expressed in your wines. However, I never recommend having more than a handful of different importers. To appoint more than that comes with a dizzying array of issues and obstacles I'll go into later.

LinkedIn

This can be a useful resource or a minefield of lost opportunities. It is a business tool for a member of any industry and again depends on to what degree you are willing to put in some effort, research and consider the source of many of the solicitations you'll find there from people who are "looking for wines from..." Are they legitimate? Are they appropriately licensed to import? This is another instance where you utilize the skills and knowledge you're acquiring to ascertain whether this is a viable avenue. Anyone can create a website, profile or presence on the Internet. Many of those who do are exactly what they purport to be; some are not.

Not too long ago, someone posted a 'new discussion' on a LinkedIn group, saying they were an importer looking for all sorts of wines from a variety of regions to fulfill the needs of a vast distributor network in the United States. Everything was in place; they just needed the wine. Already this was a red flag to me.

- Who has a built-in network and no product?
- If they had such a network, how was this achieved?
- Why would they need to issue a very broad, blanket invitation in a group, instead of being more specific?
- How did they generate a distribution network when they had only been in business, at that time, for one month?

As the posts from interested wineries started piling up from all over the world, there were no more posts from this so-called importer. He had disappeared. Although I had no personal or professional interest in the business or the outcome, I was concerned for what I felt to be naïve wineries, all hoping for a piece of this distribution pie.

Very often something that seems too good is. At the request of another LinkedIn member who was the LinkedIn group administrator, I began to research the company on the internet and could find nothing—no website, mention of an event, reference to distributor, nothing. There was an apparent wholesale business that had been established at a time that coincided with the date of the original post, but that was all. Someone who is supposedly so tapped into the country's wine distribution and planned to import should at least have a rudimentary website. This begins to build a picture of who the importer is, their background, expertise, experience, aspirations and so forth. It's a place to start and from which to build.

Some time later, I was contacted by a brand owner who had sent samples to this 'importer', which had apparently been held up at customs and returned, at great expense, to the country of origin. The brand owner thought they were doing the right thing by having a conversation with this individual and asking for a copy of their import license. Unfortunately, he had no idea what an import license looked like and what other questions to ask. I requested a copy to verify what he'd been sent, which turned out to be a local business license and did not resemble an importer license in any way. It would have been useless in clearing samples through U.S. Customs. There was no further contact from the 'importer' and the brand owner learned a hard lesson.

On the other hand, I saw a discussion posting from a wine producer that said this:

"Dear all, we are looking for a capable F&B distributor in USA. It is essential that the distributor is already present in the best hotels and resorts in America."

This posting went on to say that their product was positioned in the "Luxury Market" and wished to remain that way. It was another classic example of someone, or a company, that has done little or no research on the U.S. market. First of all, they were looking for an "F&B distributor", not an importer. Secondly, whatever is taking place in other parts of the world for their product, real or imagined, has no bearing on what will happen in the United States. Thirdly, competition for that segment of the market is very stiff and often predicated on connections, reputation and previous history. Expecting to penetrate it at the introduction is quite often a misguided view.

This is not at all a criticism of LinkedIn. On the contrary, I find it to be a valuable professional resource and I unexpectedly found a distributor on there a few years ago. The difference is that I knew the right questions to ask and the distributor demonstrated that they were a legitimate and trustworthy company. As a winery, exporter or brand owner, the way to utilize the LinkedIn community effectively is to make sure that you word the post in such a way that it demonstrates at least a rudimentary understanding of the U.S. wine industry, provide succinct and appealing points about your wines, appear professional and know how to evaluate the responses.

Other Connections

Although we have covered many more focused ways to locate and vet an importer, do not discount the value of word-of-mouth recommendations and networking. Again, the analogy of a job search or executive position appointment is apt. Sometimes, networking through your winery and vineyard friends, barrel suppliers, shippers, brokers and local organization resources provide a wealth of contacts. Your search may not end with the first person you speak with, nor the first importer they recommend, but if you have ever been a job seeker, can you remember how you contacted a recommendation, who referred you to the next? Being able to offer a mutually known name to that next unknown but recommended company representative opens doors. The implied endorsement endows the experience with a sense of familiarity and a certain comfort level.

* * *

Final Thoughts

In the beginning of my career, I was full of enthusiasm, determined to offer the best representation to any winery that I could and work hard to become worthy of that trust. However, without any mentor or information about importing available, I was really operating in a vacuum. I was prone to naiveté and pitfalls. Initially, I brought in a wine that didn't sell because it was not suited to the American palate, accepted wines with excessive pricing and tolerated packaging that turned off even the most interested potential customers. There is no reason to eliminate an importer based on their lack of experience, if that is your choice, because they can often be your most ardent fan and will work hard to build the portfolio. But always make the decision with awareness of their limitations and ability. Your understanding of the U.S. market, hopefully made through this book and other research, will be one of your best assets and can help both you and your importer in your venture.

Whether it is a trade show, wine fair, website search or someone who responds to your email, it is absolutely essential to the success of your quest that you conduct your own research and vetting. And never send samples unless you have made personal contact and have determined that there is serious interest.

In the recent past, I received a box of wine out of the blue from Spain (see Figure 9). I hadn't agreed to receive samples from them and was unaware it was coming. I still have no idea who identified me as a target or cleared the samples through customs for this purpose.

Inside, there were six beautifully packaged wines from different regions with each bottle encased in a decorated metal cylinder. There was also a heavy, expensive looking coffee table size, hardcover, full-color book. And a folder of marketing material. I leafed through the book. Gorgeous, artful photos of vineyards, wineries, landscape, bottles, food. With almost no words. What was I supposed to take from this? I read the accompanying letter. I was curious so I went to the website referenced in the letter, where there was an invitation to a "virtual tasting" without accountability

Figure 9 **Unsolicited samples from Spain**

or stated purpose. To this day, I still don't know what it was about, because no one contacted me to enlighten me.

Perhaps other recipients of this wine were so impressed by this extravagant marketing exercise they immediately signed up to be importers and distributors. Perhaps they saw the marketing as sophisticated and edgy. Perhaps they understood more about it than I did. I was simply mystified. They had made some crucial mistakes with me:

- They did not identify whether I was importing new wines
- They did not identify whether I was interested in importing from Spain
- They did not identify me by name
- They provided no compelling reason or purpose for the samples
- They did not follow up in any way

Eventually I drank the wines, which were actually quite good. I threw out the marketing materials. I recycled the metal tubes and I kept the book. I'm a book lover. I can't bring myself to dispose of something so beautifully produced. It's collecting dust on my office shelf.

Focus, specificity and knowing your audience is key to outreach for a winery or wine region organization. An email can work if some research and preparation is conducted beforehand and the communication is personalized and compelling. A personal contact to determine (a) if samples are welcome and (b) the desired outcome, would be advisable. And follow up is essential.

5

Exploring Options

Part of the process of finding a U.S. importer is trying to anticipate what will attract one, and laying the appropriate foundation towards a successful partnership. Aside from the obvious wine quality and pricing issues, I can tell you from experience that any U.S. importer would prefer to deal with a prepared and personable supplier, who either demonstrates some business savvy or is willing to defer to someone who does. This is not always possible, as we all know, but flexibility, tamping down the ego and being willing to listen, not dictate, is also paramount. No one wants to take on a brand, only to find out that you will be expending too much energy disabusing the owner of false or outmoded ideas, battling with egos or being completely misunderstood because of a language barrier. There will sometimes be language barriers to overcome, hoops to jump through and a good deal of difficulty in coming to terms with the convoluted U.S. rules and regulations, but that is expected. The U.S. is not an easy country in which to do business. And many brand owners are farmers at heart who would rather be out in the vineyard than negotiating a business deal. However, I would prefer to deal with an affable brand owner who is new to the market but intends to become educated about it than represent an exclusive, highly rated brand if it also means having to deal with the officious, obstinate brand owner that comes with it! In the end, this is not a relationship that is going to work, for either side.

An Export Broker/Agent

Either "broker" or "agent" is used in this context to mean a role within your country, not the U.S. I use "broker" in this section for consistency, but you may know it as an export agent. A winery from any foreign country may find and begin working directly with a U.S. importer, but in the event that language is such a barrier that it cannot be overcome simply with Google translation, it might be an opportunity to find a broker within your own country to become the go-between. This individual will charge a commission or fee of course, but could be someone who finds or recommends an importer for you through their familiarity with the United States and representing other wineries.

A commission is the broker's bread and butter after all, which they make either directly from you or by adding a markup to the wine, in a price quoted to the importer. If your wines are price sensitive, any additional costs may be a problem, but an export broker can often be worth it. These are some or all of the functions they can perform, depending upon the country and your needs:

- They should be very familiar with your region and comparable brands, thereby cutting down on some of the potential for excessive travel and time commitment through their effective communication with the importer.

- They should be reasonably fluent, or at least conversant, in English and presumably have an established reputation or relationship with other brands as a broker. Even English-speaking Australia, South Africa and New Zealand have their distinct customs, idioms and idiosyncrasies and an export agent may well be an advantage in bridging the gap with the importer.

- They should be familiar with shipping logistics and able to send samples on your behalf for the importer to evaluate.

- Brokers are also often much more familiar with the U.S. requirements than wineries and can be your intermediary in communicating these to you from the importer, with a knowledgeable foundation from having done the same thing before.

- They are in a position to convey expectations from you to the importer and vice versa.

- Brokers may be able to help negotiate pricing, based on their understanding of your wines, or a familiarity with comparable wines and market conditions. Although you probably have a certain price you are accustomed to receiving for the wines, sometimes the price is influenced by exchange rates and U.S. margins and market expectations. Of course, the ultimate decision is up to you, as the exporter and/or brand owner, but a small adjustment could mean the difference between a purchase or not.
- A broker will presumably have experience with freight forwarders and shipping companies, which ports to use and even container consolidation of wines, thereby relieving you of the headache of such arrangements.

In evaluating a broker relationship, it is important to weigh the added cost of the agent and the distance it can create between you and the importer, against your time and resources and your familiarity with these aspect and ability to handle them yourself. By distance, I am referring to a detachment from your importer, whereby you are not engaged in building a relationship because the agent is the one conducting business. I am not making a recommendation either way; I am only pointing out the intangible costs that are sometimes incurred. When these are weighed against the benefits of facilitating communication, logistics and sales, only you will know whether it is worthwhile.

As with any field, there are good and bad brokers, which should become readily apparent in the early stages of your association. There are also those who are just plain insecure and will try to be an unnecessary buffer between you and the importer, out of fear you will cut them out of the transaction when the importer has established the brand. Their fear may be unfounded, but I would like to point out that you should never do that. It's not ethical. Honor whatever arrangement you agreed upon, and have a contract if necessary, and spell out the term limits of your affiliation.

Just as essentially, you should want to establish your own relationship with the importer. The more interaction you have with the importer and the more you support their efforts, the more they will regard your brand as an important component of their portfolio. If they know and like you, they will be more concerned with your needs and building a long-term commitment to your brand.

A broker does not need to be someone who becomes entangled in your affairs to any great degree. They may simply be someone you contract with for certain arrangements, such as to facilitate logistics, coordinate shipments, assist with label compliance and communicate with the importer to help time-sensitive events proceed more smoothly. This is only an option, not a requirement. Aside from their facility with language, consider the time you have to devote to the U.S. as an export market, whether you are part of a consortium of wineries that have banded together to find U.S. representation, and the caliber of a broker. A good, experienced broker could make a big difference in being able to lay the groundwork and allowing you to avoid that steep learning curve you would otherwise face.

Awards, Medals, Ratings

These are often far less significant than you may think, but still part of your arsenal. Many winery owners will point proudly to the bronze medal they were awarded at the local wine fair, the three stars they garnered in an obscure publication or accolades from the home town wine stores. And of course they should be proud. These are barometers of the wine's desirability and worth on a national level in their own country. Unfortunately, they mean very little to the U.S. industry professional or consumer.

There are always exceptions to every rule. If the gold medal is from a show that has international recognition, the rating is in a publication such as Decanter, published in about ninety countries and widely available in the U.S., James Halliday's Wine Companion (Australia), or Michael Cooper's Buyer's Guide (New Zealand), or recommended by Master of Wine and renowned writer, Jancis Robinson (UK), then the rules are slightly different, because they are known and respected in the U.S. Something like Vinum Magazine, despite being widely read throughout parts of Europe, is virtually unknown here. Sadly, none of these ultimately replace the U.S. ratings anyway, but they are a providential boost to the wine in the early days, a reasonable precursor of how well it will do when it does appear in a U.S. publication and an immediate marketing tool. Winemaker of the Year or some other significant designation is also an evaluation gauge for a potential importer.

If you don't have any outside recognition for your wines or the vineyard, I suggest submitting to researched publications and well regarded shows in your country or region. If you have distribution in any other countries, perhaps there is something to use from there. These are not essential channels, but until you achieve U.S. distribution you will not be able to submit to most U.S. publications, so there is some value in other types of regional press. (The exception to this would be *Wine Advocate* (Robert Parker) which does not accept unsolicited samples, but does enter wines into their data base for consideration. If selected, *Wine Advocate* sends out a call for entries when a brand's region is due to be reviewed in the publication.) It is also a valuable barometer for you. If certain wines do consistently well and others do not, this may be the time for your own reevaluation before you make your presentation to a potential U.S. importer.

Cellar Door Visits

If you are fortunate enough to have a cellar door or tasting room attached to your winery or vineyard in a well-traveled area then you may have international visitors who come by and try your wines, including those from the United States. This is an initial opportunity to start to build demand and an avenue to U.S. export. It is important to add that not everyone from the U.S. in the wine trade who professes love for your wine will have any influence, nor will they necessarily think your wines have sales viability. It is not that they are simply being polite. Anyone who appears enthusiastic probably is, or it is hardly worth the time to make such a fuss. If they take your card or give you their contact details it will be because they are sufficiently impressed with the wines to want to be advised when they are available in the U.S. But a local wine shop in a small town in the States, for example, cannot legally bring in your wines and is unlikely to have connections to an importer who can.

However, there are retail *chain* buyers who not only have considerable influence, they also have their own 'clearing' import companies should they wish to bring in wines. An importer who clears wines for a retail chain is still very much a fully licensed and federally regulated business, but they will often agree to bring in wines the chain has chosen for their stores for a nominal fee. It must also go through a distributor (which may be the same entity), and must be handled and warehoused at the wholesale distributor's premises before being shipped to the retailer. This is the three-tier system in action.

The point is that the right retail chain has the ability to bring in pallets or even a full container of wine it selects. This could become an option for you in your quest to export to the U.S., keeping in mind that the wine will only go to that one retail store chain, wherever its distribution may be, and not distributed throughout the States. Nor will the wine be in restaurants. It is, however, a wonderful first step and may be where you want to begin and end. Financial stability is virtually guaranteed, plus a steady supply of orders. But it will also be dependent on the tastes of the chain buyer at that time, which may change. I'll discuss more in a later chapter on how to support, grow and generally capitalize on this option. Regardless of where it leads, it is still an excellent way to lay a foundation for the present, and

Figure 10 Murdoch James cellar door

attract an importer who can provide you with broader market distribution later.

Let me be clear that I know not everyone has a cellar door (Figure 10), tasting room or even an accessible vineyard. Wine regions are many and varied throughout the world and often the decision to establish a brand does not necessarily follow any well-trodden path. I have encountered and represented many variations. Brands come about through a winemaker's evolution working at a winery and desire to have his or her own brand on which to put their stamp. It may start by sourcing grapes from a friend's vineyard and making it in a garagiste environment where a number of winemakers are sharing a spartan space to produce their own wine. Or sourcing grapes from specific vineyards in larger quantities for special wines that have a sense of terroir but no actual home. I used to visit a winemaker whose uncle provided a section of his old vines vineyard for the winemaker's exclusive use, and he made the wines in an historic, but very small, falling down cottage, over 100 years old, where we had to climb over the barrels to get to a cramped working space in the middle of the room. Nonetheless, the wines were worth the effort for both him to make and me to import.

Possibly the region is so remote that there are no visitors. These are all normal circumstances for wine brands and not obstacles. If you finally decide you have sufficient volume and motivation to export then consider where your wines may already be sold that could attract attention or visitors from the U.S. Does the hotel or restaurant have a high profile in the area? Do they have connections in the U.S.? What about the other wines on their list? If these wines already have an importer, it may be the way you can piggyback to representation. This is an opportunity to contact that importer and tell them you share a wine list with the same wines they represent.

There are many creative ways to go about finding a U.S. importer and if you're willing to think outside the box they can be extremely productive.

* * *

Final Thoughts

I once imported a brand whose entire operation, including multiple country export logistics, took place in a stone house. In the kitchen, where the bookkeeper did her work at the counter, she had to move when someone opened the refrigerator. Today, this same brand is a multi-million dollar operation where their wine is made in a gleaming state-of-the-art facility, complete with restaurant, conference rooms and workout gym. They employed a gifted winemaker who didn't compromise on quality and made superb wines, but much of the brand's early success can absolutely be attributed to sales in the U.S., from ratings in U.S. publications and through the winemaker's outlandish personality and forward thinking. Sales in the U.S. built this brand into an icon that created demand in other countries, including the winemaker's own country, from the prestige of what had been accomplished in the U.S.

Not only thinking outside the box in a quest for U.S. representation, but being willing to explore unconventional avenues to the same goal, or perhaps looking at an option to which you have some resistance, can often be more successful than treading the well-worn path of those who have gone before you. Along those lines, I also believe there is value in an old English proverb that says you can be "penny wise and pound foolish". In other words, by not securing an export broker (if you really need one), or refusing to negotiate on pricing, or foregoing other expenses, you may save money in the short term but lose valuable sales income in the long term.

Part II

6

The Courtship

Narrowing the Field
At this point it is about sorting through prospects and deciding who, how and what to pursue. I think by now you know what I'm going to say: this is a decision that must be carefully made. It is a commitment leading to a long-term relationship. To treat it any other way is a complete waste of your time, effort and money. This is something I will continue to emphasize throughout the book. Applying yourself diligently to the pursuit of an importing partnership in the United States is the only way to ensure establishing your brand, rather than just making a sale.

The Personalities
Using the different means laid out in previous chapters, there should be a number of importers that look like good candidates and you may think that personality is the least of the criteria.

"It's all about business," you might say, but it's so much more than that; it's a relationship. There are many more relationships you will develop throughout the sales and distribution of your wines, but this is clearly one of the most important. So, consider your personality and what type of person you are likely to work well with for the long-term. Are you:

- Driven
- Goal oriented
- Focused
- Detail oriented
- Opposed to deadlines imposed by others
- Workaholic
- Responsive to requests
- Laid back
- Communicative
- Collaborative

This would be the time to consider whether you can work with the autocratic, new importer who retired from a senior position with Microsoft and cashed out his stock to start an import business, but who retains that Type A tendency to require perfection from himself and everyone around him. Are *you* the retired or cashed-out executive before you planted your vineyard who understands exactly how he feels and is a perfect fit? Are you accepting of this importer's need for direct and constant communication on new vintage releases or shipment timing, a self-assurance that sufficient due diligence on the competition has yielded an exact pricing algorithm, and expectation that you must contribute significantly to the U.S. enterprise including a semi-annual trip to work the market?

Or are you the local, reclusive winemaker, who makes wines utilizing what the *terroir* gives you that vintage—and it's very good—but you don't know a graph from a graft and really aren't interested. You just want to make your 800 to 1,000 cases of wine—depending upon the year—and find good homes for them. If the importer doesn't commit to the wine quickly enough, it may be sold elsewhere, because it's all the same to you, and you most likely won't come over to visit, because you can't afford to and the dogs would miss you. But you won't compromise on quality and will supply your importer with whatever they need, *as long as they speak up quickly because it may be sold to someone else.* There are importers in the U.S. who not only understand and appreciate this type of mentality, but seek it out and thrive on it.

These might sound like extremes or caricatures, and of course they are largely composite examples for the sake of illustrating my point, but I can assure you I know people exactly like this, and countless other different, but equally quirky, challenging, interesting, entertaining, frustrating and ultimately extremely rewarding wine trade people. The issue is whether you can work with a particular personality type and who best suits your style. Can you modify yours, and they theirs, and meet somewhere in the middle? Occasionally, it's not so much about the style, as the character traits. If the individual is purely ego driven, greedy and untrustworthy, it doesn't matter how much they promise you, whether they are male or female, market savvy or blithely naive. Inevitably, this will become a nightmare and you will regret the decision to override your instinctive reaction.

Expectations—Yours and Theirs

Beyond personalities and working styles, it becomes imperative to establish in the early stages what the expectations are on both sides. Leave no aspect to chance and assume nothing. Without this caveat, you would be surprised at the extent of resources that can be spent on securing an importer, only to become aware of a deal breaking requirement on their part, or an assumption on yours that was never addressed. Some of these might be:

- National vs. regional appointment
- Terms
- Which wines
- First year volume
- Allocation

National vs. Regional

Since national and regional importing are so different, and critical to your own vision for the future of the brand, it is in your best interests to determine from the start of your business which model works best for you or whether it's possible to adapt to an importer's territory because they have demonstrated they are a good fit in every other way.

National Representation

A national importer means assigning to them exclusive rights for the entire country. They will be based in one state and from there they can appoint wholesalers in each state *in which they can secure distribution*. I emphasize that last part because this hinges on the relationships and connections this importer has and how appealing your wines are to the people this importer contacts. There is no guarantee that having exclusive rights to all fifty states means that they will have distribution in all fifty states, but it could mean they intend to—an important distinction. It also depends on how much effort the importer puts into working the market to achieve results and any number of other variables. Here are some pros and cons to consider:

Pros

- A cohesive approach to U.S. sales
- Your importer has free rein to seek out and find distribution
- One importer to communicate with and receive reports and feedback
- No overlap or confusion on submitting wines to publication, events and rating opportunities
- One point person for any chain business that crosses state lines
- The opportunity to develop a stronger relationship with your importer
- An importer who does not have to worry about his or her competition in other parts of the country and takes this as a challenge to do more
- Allocations are able to be consistently monitored and maintained through one source
- No conflicts developing over allocations, sales territories or opposing visions

Cons

- All eggs are in one basket—that is, the success of the brand rides on one person
- The lack of competition with other regions may mean less motivation to increase sales at a dynamic rate
- The importer may not be the best fit after all, only apparent after the exclusive appointment

- The importer may be new and lacking in the right connections, which will be overcome in time, but is an initial impediment to launching the brand
- If resources are limited, or become stretched, traveling the entire country and monitoring all distribution may become difficult

Regional Importers

If you are considering appointing regional importers, assuming you have the option by virtue of demand and opportunity, the pros and cons might look like this:

Pros

- Allowing different states or territorial importer to develop their own sales within a familiar area
- Smaller geographical area more easily controlled and monitored through travel and greater communication
- Competition between importers can be a healthy stimulus to sales
- Diversifying through the appointment of more than one importer provides the opportunity to take advantage of different strengths and connections
- Allows you to see whether opposition to a wine style, packaging design or price point is the perception of one individual or a consensus
- If one or more importers' sales are insufficient, there are others to make up this shortfall
- Allows you to see if someone is not working out and either redistributing regions or giving notice to the importer, knowing that sales are still being made in other areas

Cons

- Wasted exercises in duplicate submitting to events, publications and rating sources
- The converse result that nothing is submitted, because each importer thought someone else was doing it
- Potential for conflict with pricing and approach to markets

- Significant potential for conflict in the event that one importer has established business with a chain that overlaps into other importers' territories in terms of compensation and control
- Undercutting business
- Over-selling beyond allocations, resulting in shortages in other regions or dissatisfied customers

As with all pros and cons I lay out, and any issues where there is a decision to make, it is simply something to factor into your thought processes. There is no one avenue to representation, and often it comes down to which present the best prospects. Whichever route you wish to take or have the opportunity to secure - national distribution through one importer or multiple importers to diversify and spread the risk - this should be discussed in the beginning to avoid misunderstanding or potentially to influence either party to make another choice.

Terms

This can be a tricky issue, because you may be accustomed to selling, for example, to China, a market where customarily payment is made prior to shipping product, or within Europe, where it may be upon receipt of goods.

In the U.S., although they vary, common U.S. terms for wine purchase are anywhere from 60 to 120 days from B/L (Bill of Lading), FOB (Freight on Board) port of origin. In other words, the winery gets the wine to the port nearest to them, or the one nearest to them that ships to the U.S., and the date on the B/L provided by the shipping company is when the clock starts ticking. This lessens the time where wine is sitting at the dock waiting for a ship.

It would not be unreasonable to expect payment for a first shipment when it leaves port or arrives in the U.S. or under LC (Letter of Credit) to ensure payment. This requires a guarantee from the importer, through a letter from their bank, to ensure sufficient funds will be on deposit to pay the invoice at the close of terms. Initially, this should be perfectly acceptable, especially if the importer is new or quite small. There are also instances where one-half is due upon shipment and one-half on receipt, but keep in mind that payment terms are not an immutable facet of a U.S. wine purchase and if you feel there are other factors that weigh in favor of extending terms, then by all means do so. Terms can always be redrawn at a later date.

My caveat to you is not to be so focused on getting a sale in the U.S. that you forget that the primary goal is to be *paid* for the sale. If you extend terms and they seem to be abused, or you have a sense that finances are becoming a concern, it is entirely your prerogative to require a tighter rein on payment. To do otherwise under those circumstances is to invite greater financial exposure for you.

Which Wines
As a vineyard, brand or winery owner, with a quiver full of varietals of which you are justly proud, you might expect the importer to take them all. It will be up to the potential importer to explain that whilst they are all lovely in their own inimitable ways, the ones they feel best equipped to begin with, based on market research, style, price, or whatever the reason, are, for example, "these three wines". It may not be the conventional varietals that win over the esoteric or funky. It could be that *that* style of Merlot from Pemberton, Australia won't sell, or the Bordeaux blend from Gimblett Gravels, New Zealand will be too difficult at that price point. They may be beautifully made wines, with structural integrity and recognizable grape names, but if it doesn't appear to be the right time, then don't expect the importer to buck trends.

On the other hand, if all your wines represent enormous volume potential, value priced and over-delivering on quality, the type of importer you would be considering would most likely have existing connections to chains and full-time employees to oversee national operations. The strength of their operation still does not mean that they are likely to import everything you produce at the outset, but likelier to build across the brand in a shorter timeframe. Just remember that the market guides these purchases and may be different from tastes and styles you are accustomed to selling in Europe or Asia.

First Year Volume
This is a small sampling of actual statements made by different winery participants at VinItaly (the international wine competition held in Italy):

> "How many pallets will your first order be? We would like to see five to 10 pallets to start."
>
> "Once this wine is in the U.S. it will sell easily because it is from xxx region."
>
> "I want to have many importers so that my product is in a lot of states."
>
> "My wine has a DOC, which is well known abroad, so the wine will sell itself."

"How long till my wines are nationwide?"

All of these statements demonstrate a basic lack of knowledge about the U.S. wine industry. Initial volume is a critical element to be discussed between you and your importer, but misunderstanding is often at the root of disappointment. An informed producer is armed with knowledge and realistic expectations that provide a basis for success. In my experience, the biggest misconception of all is that because the United States is a nation of wine lovers and the population numbers over 300 million people, your paltry 5,000 cases a year would be absorbed in no time. This is when an importer tries to explain that of those multi-millions, only a certain percentage drink wine, of those a smaller percentage drink regularly and a number of people only drink very inexpensive local wines, or wines of a certain country.

Yes, U.S. wine drinking is increasing in both actual volume and annual per capita consumption and the right wine, marketed properly, can certainly export in the thousands and possibly hundreds of thousands of cases. But add to the mix the sheer volume of international imports, America's own robust wine production, increased plantings everywhere and the consolidation of wholesalers and you have a situation that requires a skillful, savvy approach. It is far better for an importer to set conservative expectations and exceed them, to your delight, than for you to have bottled and labeled all your production just for the U.S. and find yourself facing financial ruin. My statements here, as throughout the entire book, are not to discourage you but to suggest that this must be viewed and approached as a business proposition, with all the knowledge and tools you will need at your disposal before you begin.

Most importers will necessarily need to start slowly, to establish the brand carefully and not overwhelm distributors. Fostering a warm and collaborative relationship is crucial, but this is *their* business and they must purchase according to common sense and fiscal constraints. It is also a guide to you as to which importer might be best suited to represent your brand and which vision more closely matches your own. Again, a caveat: don't be blinded by what you want. Trust that a good, experienced importer will know what will be most likely to succeed and that a new, inexperienced importer is going to start slowly and add carefully as the market dictates.

Allocation

Although the early stages are all about lowered expectations and conservative commitments, you still want to consider how much you are willing to allocate to the U.S. overall, and to each importer if you have more than one. If you have an almost limitless supply and allocations are not really an issue, then this is simply about planning how to commit resources to your new export market. But if your vineyard is a special place of old vines that produces only 300 cases of each wine in a vintage, it is very important to communicate to your U.S. importer whether they can have 290 cases or 50 and whether this is a fluid allocation or static. If the wines garner amazing press or achieve cult status this will become even more critical for your importer's planning, and if you are splitting the country you will need to make sure that the wines are split fairly with the other importer. Do not confuse allocation with *commitment*, unless you want it to mean the same thing. You can let the importer know this is the amount you will allocate to the U.S., but requiring a sales commitment from them is something else entirely.

Background Checking

I'm not actually suggesting that you investigate your potential importer. But requesting references would be perfectly acceptable as you evaluate their company's financial stability and whether they are new or not. Length of time in business is not necessarily a barometer of asset strength. New importers will certainly be under the microscope more because there is no history, but well established importers can overextend themselves, as many have done, and be in a precarious financial position. Bank and funding source references will help establish a foundation for the new importer and vendor references—other brands, trucking, shipping and warehousing businesses - will be important for the more established company.

* * *

Final Thoughts

My experience has mostly been as a national importer with responsibility for the entire country as opposed to a proscribed geographical region. I will be honest and say that I much preferred it that way, because I could pick and choose which states to go into irrespective of their geographic proximity to any other state or region and could go at my own pace according to my own business plan. However, as I stated in the body of the chapter, there were pros and cons to this scenario, both for me and the producers.

As a small company it could sometimes be difficult to cover the entire country, because my wholesalers were located in pockets across the entire U.S. but not necessarily in concentrated regions. It was expensive to visit them all in a reasonable timeframe and perhaps I could have done a better job at times. But I was also free to strategize, to capitalize on connections I made at trade shows and through recommendations and to react quickly. I did not have to worry about what another importer was doing, or whether we would be stepping on each other's toes.

On the other hand, I had one supplier of two brands who was convinced that a larger, better-financed importer in New York could do a superior job and, whilst I was doing reasonably well, he was sure his wines would set the world on fire if only they were in more prestigious hands. They never did go on to "set the world on fire". In fact, the prestigious importer in New York placed one order, the brands languished in their crowded portfolio and eventually disappeared. Neither brand has ever reappeared in the U.S.

The summary for this chapter is really about the continuing subjectivity of any situation between exporter and importer, and that there is no "one size fits all" in the process. For anyone to suggest otherwise is to ignore the variables of personalities, work styles and prevailing circumstances. As you have already gathered, I am not proposing that it is easy to find a U.S. importer and that you can pick and choose among a range of potential candidates, but never settle for a poor fit and once you do find one importer—or more than one—it is still up to each of you to find common ground and optimum conditions for the best possible outcome.

7

The Engagement

Once you and the importer have made the decision to enter into this relationship, the real work begins. The following are relatively small concerns after the large issues you sorted through to reach an accord, but sooner or later they must be dealt with. I like to get them all on the table so that you have as detailed a picture as possible from the beginning. Some of them arise during the evaluation stage, but it makes more sense to group them with the practical aspects of your new relationship, rather than with the much broader issues and discretionary outcomes we tackled in the last chapter.

Samples
At some point in the process, the prospective importer will want sample bottles to evaluate and perhaps taste with others for their opinions. It doesn't matter whether an importer has tasted through your lineup at your vineyard or has never met you or tasted your wines. If they express interest in receiving samples, it is presumably because they are serious about representation and tasting the samples is a necessary part of the process. Even if all wines have been tasted with you, it is most likely that they will

want to taste them away from the influence of the ambiance of the vineyard and emotion of the moment. And taste them over a day or two back in the States and possibly with people whose opinions they value.

Samples are expensive to send, so you must strike a balance between too many and too little. If you have dozens of different wines in your brand you can't send them all and most likely many of them won't be marketable. You might want to sell all of them, but this is not realistic and the importer will decide which have the best chance of a successful launch. Input from you will be valuable, especially if your prospective importer has not tasted the wines. An insignificant remaining inventory of a current vintage will not be relevant; it's the next vintage that needs to be evaluated. Describe the styles. If it is a sweet, late harvest Syrah, obviously this needs to be disclosed, rather than allowing the importer to think they are receiving a dry table wine Shiraz.

Legally, there is virtually no limit to the number of samples of diverse wines that can be sent, within reason. U.S. Customs and Border Protection does not seek to legislate how many different wines an importer can evaluate, but if it is a large number of bottles of the same wine, TTB may ask the importer to justify its use. Logically, with a view to the expense you are incurring, it is a matter of balancing the number of wines you ship with the opportunity for sufficient quantity to provide broad assessment for your prospective customer. Additionally, if you plan on sending only one sample of each wine, I strongly recommend shipping two bottles of each if you are using cork. There is no point in sending one bottle of a corked wine with no opportunity to properly estimate its value to an importer's portfolio.

Sample Bottle Requirements

This would be a good place to mention that, in addition to the paperwork the winery must complete to consign the samples to the importer—an airway bill that lists importer contact details, the contents of the case(s), importer license numbers, and detailed contents of the shipment—a winery/shipper must also label each bottle, as per the waiver letter mentioned in the first chapter, with the following three items:

1. Sample Only—Not for Sale
2. Contains Sulfites
3. Mandatory Health Warning (which looks like this)

GOVERNMENT WARNING: *(1) According to the Surgeon General, women should not drink alcoholic beverages during pregnancy because of the risk of birth defects. (2) Consumption of alcoholic beverages impairs your ability to drive a car or operate machinery, and may cause health problems.*

If Customs chooses to inspect a shipment and these statements are not on the bottles, it will either destroy the goods or return them to the sender.

FDA Registrations

It is at the point of sending samples that you will need to register with the FDA (Food and Drug Administration) www.fda.gov. This can be a very confusing process for wineries, since there is no mention of wine on their site when you are looking for facility registrations. Wine comes under the heading of a "food facility". Further compounding confusion is the requirement to assign a U.S. registered agent as part of this process. Although you are still in the early stages of determining whether an importer will be taking on your brand, assigning the recipient of the samples as your agent to satisfy this requirement should not cause you any concern. As part of protecting U.S. borders against terrorist attacks and contamination of the food chain, FDA requires that any "food" entering the United States is tracked through this registration, whether or not it is for actual commerce. That is, if the samples are purely for use as samples for trade shows and evaluation by potential importers. Therefore, you must assign a U.S. agent who presumably is willing to act as your U.S. representative in the event of contact by an FDA agent. This is non-binding and can be revised by you at any time you wish. However, in this instance it is the best option to facilitate the process.

The following are some of the most salient requirements, directly from the FDA site, among the many questions they address.

Q What information must the U.S. agent have on the foreign facility? For example, does the U.S. agent need to know and understand the company and product? Or is it sufficient for the U.S. agent to be able to contact the manufacturer quickly in case of emergency, as well as serve as a conduit for the general information flow to and from FDA?

A Under 21 CFR 1.227(b)(13), there are two qualifications for a U.S. agent. The agent (1) must reside or maintain a place of business in the U.S. and (2) must be physically present in the U.S. Although the U.S. agent is not required to know and understand the facility's company and product, the U.S. agent must be able to serve as the communication link between FDA and the foreign facility because FDA will contact the foreign facility's U.S. agent when an emergency occurs (unless the registration specifies another emergency contact). Thus, at a minimum, the U.S. agent needs to know whom to contact at the facility if any emergency arises.

Q I am a foreign facility that does business with several different brokers. May I use more than one of these as my U.S. agent?

A No. Under 21 CFR 1.227(b), each foreign facility is required to have only one U.S. agent for food facility registration purposes. However, having a single U.S. agent for FDA registration purposes does not preclude a facility from having multiple brokers for other business purposes. A foreign facility is not required to conduct all of its business in the U.S. through the U.S. agent designated for purposes of registration.

Q May a foreign facility appoint one U.S. agent for part of the year and another U.S. agent for the rest of the year?

A Yes. However, any change in a facility's U.S. agent must be communicated to FDA through an update of the registration information within 60 days of the change (21 CFR 1.234).

Q How does a foreign facility "authorize" someone in the U.S. to be their agent (for example, letter to FDA, notarized document)?

A From FDA's perspective, for registration purposes, listing the name and contact information for the U.S. agent in the registration is sufficient to "authorize" the agent. For its own business reasons, however, a facility may want to formalize its relationship with the agent with some sort of written agreement. Regardless of whether there is a formalized relationship between the facility and its U.S. agent, FDA does expect that the personnel from the facility will have verified that the person designated in the facility's registration as its U.S. agent is willing to serve as the agent.

From my own perspective and experience, FDA registrations are not difficult, but definitely need some guidance from a person who is conversant with the process, either the importer who is requesting the samples or a consultant who truly is familiar with what is required. If there is a charge for completing the registration and acting as U.S. agent it should be a manageable figure. There is no charge for the actual registration to the FDA on their website.

Additionally, changing U.S. agents, should you wish to do so at any time, is no problem and requires no authorization, notice or release from the current agent. Finally, in over twenty years as an importer, and dozens of appointments as a U.S. agent, I have never been contacted by the FDA for any reason. So although this appears a little daunting as a federal government requirement it really is just an annoying formality. One, however, that you cannot circumvent. Here is what they say about that:

Q What will happen to an article of food that is offered for import into the U.S. from a facility with an invalid registration that FDA determined to be invalid because it does not include a U.S. agent who affirmatively agreed to serve in that capacity?

A When FDA determines that the registration for a foreign food facility is invalid because it does not provide a U.S. agent, FDA will hold shipments offered for import from that facility at the U.S. border until the facility amends their registration to list a U.S. agent who has affirmatively agreed to serve as such.

Contracts

I have rarely had a contract with a winery, but this is a product of starting my own import business in 1992 when contracts were not common, and because this has traditionally been an industry of handshake agreements. However, based on experience, and that of others, I *do* recommend a contract of some sort - a simple, but comprehensive, agreement that covers responsibilities and expectations - the salient points of your working partnership. I would be careful of prolonging the process, and possibly delaying getting started, with a league of attorneys taking weeks to construct a document that takes weeks for each side to decipher. I find that the more complicated it gets with greater protections shrouded in legalese, the less likely it is to be a satisfactory arrangement. That sounds counterintuitive, but that is my experience. The only time I had a business partner in all these years of importing, we began with more agreements and contracts than I've ever seen in my life, all signed in the office of his attorney. It did nothing to promote a successful partnership. The most harmonious relationships I have ever had were when trust was inherent on both sides. Although I'm still advocating some sort of contractual agreement for clarity and peace of mind on both sides, don't get hung up on minor details. Experience has taught me that a contract is only as good as the people who signed it.

On a more positive note, I believe that a reasonable contract protects both importer and brand owner, although it would depend upon each view of an agreement and individual expertise or experience in the matter. You will want assurances that the importer will pay you, of course, and available recourse in the event they do not. Most significantly, a contract should define, in written form, the areas you have already agreed upon and leave little to subjective interpretation and potential conflict. I am not an attorney, and would not presume to advise you as such, but simply put: a contract should include what you intend to provide for the importer and what they agree to do for you. I will expand on these roles in a later section so that you have a clearer picture of just what those should be. Some expectations on either side do not have to be more than verbal acknowledgments, clearing the way for more discussion, but it allows you to incorporate those points that are most meaningful to you, and gives both sides a measure of confidence moving forward.

I try to be objective when writing from the perspective of the supplier who is looking for sound advice on how to penetrate the U.S. wine market. This book, after all, is directed at you and your success may well depend upon the extent to which you follow my advice. But I am also mindful that there are other parties in this relationship. Any contract should also afford the importer some protection in the event you decide to change importers after they have built the brand's sales and distribution to a measurable degree of success. This has been accomplished through their considerable efforts and deserves some compensation. Nonetheless, the brand owner is always that—the brand *owner*. The importer has agreed to be your agent in the U.S., but at no time do they own the rights to the brand and its supply and distribution. It can be taken from them at any time, irrespective of a verbal understanding. Therefore, if you are leaving for greener pastures and not because the importer has been dishonest or jeopardized your brand, compensation for future earnings is reasonable. And I stress *reasonable*. The beginning of this relationship should ideally be on a congenial footing, and one in which each party feels they are being justly represented by the contract.

Sample Allowance

A sample allowance will be familiar to most suppliers but, for the sake of clarity, in the U.S. this refers to either an allocation of free wine to the U.S. importer to be included with their order or a discount on their order intended to offset the importer's expense for sample usage. This is a significant issue that you may or may not have considered, depending upon your experience with different markets. It is one which can have a major impact on your net profit, your importer's net profits and the ability or willingness for your importer to utilize samples to increase sales.

In my opinion, any supplier of wine—vineyard or winery—should provide a sample allowance, even if your production is small. The smaller the production, the less wine is available for sale and I can understand some resistance to the concept of providing a sample allowance in that situation. But the lower the output, the smaller the sample allowance, especially if it is based on a percentage of the order. If you are expecting results, and long term relationships in the U.S., it is vital to understand how the market works and, if you understand the importance of sample usage at all stages of brand development, I believe you will more willingly provide samples as a cost of doing business.

Samples are used for many purposes but include at least the following:

- Publication and competition submission
- Prospective distributors/wholesalers evaluation
- Trade shows staffed by the distributor
- Trade shows attended by the importer
- Prospective chain buyer evaluation
- Wine dinners
- Wine tastings
- Distributor's sales meetings, where importer is meeting with sales team for the express purpose of educating them on the wines
- Distributor's sales staff for sales calls made to local accounts

A good deal of deciding what might be required or most effective is subjective, but it should prove helpful to you to know what is considered a normal range in the U.S. and how these samples will be used.

Sample allowances are usually expressed in a percentage discount off the invoice. Here are some suggestions from which you can distill what feels comfortable to you. These are all examples of allowances that I have worked with in the past:

- 5% on the first container and 2% on subsequent shipments
- 3% across the board on all shipments

- 2% across the board on all shipments, but a free case of each new wine, or new vintage, to be reviewed by press
- 5% on all new vintages, 3% on shipments of the same vintage
- 5% on new and old vintages until a satisfactory sales level is reached
- 2–5% based on cost and rarity of wine and varying with the shipment
- 2.5% across the board and free cases of unrepresented wines for your importer to evaluate, offering the advantage of pre-selling if they meet their needs

There are other permutations, but these give you the necessary springboard for your own arrangement. Now that I have explained the scope of sample usage and their absolute necessity, I am sure you can appreciate how much they are utilized in the process of establishing distribution. And remember, this is not just your investment; an importer sends out and uses far more than most sample allowances. A brand owner is simply helping the importer defray costs and giving them more latitude in utilizing samples to secure and increase sales.

Sample allowances are not to be confused with incentives. This is a separate discussion to have, including whether or not you are in a position to build incentives into the price in order to affect price and stimulate sales. Although it is a topic that may well be broached during your first negotiations with the importer, I have saved this for a later section of the book where incentives can be illustrated within the relevant framework.

Payment Currency

The question of which currency will be utilized in the payment of invoices should be raised, but there are no hard and fast rules on this. If you feel your own currency is stable and unlikely to fluctuate, or you can build in sufficient margin to allow for any such fluctuations, then it's not a problem to stay in the currency you feel most comfortable with. On the other hand, you may feel more at ease quoting in USD, building in an exchange rate cushion. Much of this depends upon discussions with the importer and where price points might be sensitive to the difference in currency quotations. You may wish to quote in USD because you have a specific retail price at which you'd like to see your wines on the shelf, such as under $10 or under $20 (both important U.S. price levels), but it is still your importer's prerogative, and the vagaries of the three-tier pricing system will have a great bearing on this, so make sure to discuss it at the outset. No one is going to benefit from incorrect assumptions.

One option for either party—supplier or purchaser—is to build in *forward contracts* with your bank or foreign exchange on currency if considerable fluctuation is already taking place or the prevailing feeling is that it is likely to increase. This demands speculation on your part and, although you have stabilized your own payment currency for the foreseeable future, it stipulates a specific currency delivery date, specific quantity of currency and at an agreed rate at the time of the contract. It locks in the rate at the current value, but requires considerable insight on your part as to your future needs.

Whatever your choice, or the importer's, factor it into your pricing and you will be better prepared in the event of instability in exchange rates and market conditions.

Pricing—In Brief

As a rule, price increases from the winery should not be automatically triggered by each vintage or the start of a new year. However, there are certainly circumstances that do precipitate an increase—for example a lower introductory price for the first shipment, unexpected costs of doing business or the winery's USD currency choice eroded by a devalued dollar.

As a supplier, you cannot anticipate some of these events, but can address, at the outset, what you anticipate will normally activate your price increases. It is not the most critical aspect of your early negotiations, but arbitrary price rises without notice and based on factors unsupported by sales in the U.S. could have potentially damaging effect on your importer's business. I mention it to inform you as to what may be customary and, to some degree, what to expect as part of the discussions to ensure your brand's optimal positioning in the U.S. market.

Short-Term Goals

My emphasis in this section is to align your goals with the importer's goals. The importer may have very specific and easily articulated ambitions that will be important for you to hear. If they do, be sure they can back them up and that you haven't been sent happily running out to buy more French oak barrels at $1,200 each based on their unsubstantiated and possibly unrealistic projections.

Some wineries only want a demonstrated effort and the assurance that the importer will take as much wine as they can sell and see what sales eventuate. This initially gives the importer a certain peace of mind, but does not guarantee supply in the long term. Since it is all part of the unknown at the outset, the importer may find themselves in the fortunate position of rapid growth, but you cannot keep up with demand because too much was left open-ended. This leaves you both with dissatisfied customers and lost sales and momentum.

On the other hand, no one can predict definitively what can be sold over a five year term, down to the last case. It is very difficult for an importer to make any projections based on no historical reference. I have often found myself in that position and I do understand the motivation behind each supplier's request for this information. After all, long range plans—and perhaps the livelihood of your entire winery family—hinge on what your export markets anticipate that sales and growth will be over time. However, I didn't want to be put in a position of committing to something on which I couldn't deliver, based on information I just don't have, and neither should your importer. I think it is reasonable to explain that you want this to be an honest and successful *long term* partnership and understand that they will be in a better position to give you their anticipated needs and objectives after the first few months or the first year.

You will at least want to ensure that in the first few months you can provide your importer with sufficient wine to back up the first orders, but don't get ahead of it and have the wines all labeled for the U.S. requirements, ready and waiting for an order. If you find this more cost-efficient, because of bottling and labeling runs, then do so by all means, but otherwise the advice I have just given should dictate how you both approach the beginning stages of this endeavor—with conservative optimism.

* * *

Final Thoughts

The best example I can think of to illustrate one of the more critical aspects of this chapter is not my story, but someone else's. A very well-known importer operated successfully in the U.S. for almost two decades, establishing small family brands and providing a level of sales these brand owners could hardly have dreamed of when he first approached them to import their wines. He made many trips to the country he sourced from to make more extravagant promises as his ego expanded. Producers readily acquiesced to his demands to add more vineyard land and infrastructure and to buy more barrels because he promised them a never-ending supply of U.S. sales to meet consumer's demands. As signs of a weakening economy became apparent, the importer ignored them; his lavish lifestyle continued unabated and the promises flowed like wine. Within two years, the importer's hubris resulted in a multi-million dollar bankruptcy. He had no reserves from which to pay his debts. Vineyard owners, wineries, freight forwarders, bottlers and coopers, who relied too heavily on him for their source of income, were now also bankrupt or near to it. Some never recovered. Others learned a very hard lesson.

Always operate within parameters you feel comfortable with and never base your financial outlays on future promises if they threaten the viability of your own business. Place a degree of trust in your importer's hands, because this is now someone you have researched, investigated and vetted, but retain control over your own business.

8

The Commitment

Now the real work begins and essentially the clock is ticking. You are responsible for meeting certain time frames and expectations and the importer is working on completing tasks at their end to set your new collaboration in motion. This is when you really start working together to get the wines sold.

American Source Letter
Federal, and some state, guidelines require your importer to prove that they have been given the rights to represent your brand in the U.S. As discussed previously, this can be an exclusive right for the whole country or can circumscribe a certain geographical area. The letter is very simple and wording is flexible, as long as you cover the main points: that you, the brand owner, have assigned a particular importer the importing rights for a certain geographical area. The letter is addressed to the importer.

In the first example, Weber Wines may have already appointed a U.S. importer for their primary brand, or have another importer appointed for other states. Therefore, the letter can look like this:

(Winery's letterhead)

Letter of Appointment as Importer of Weber Wines into the USA

(date)

(importer's name and address)

Dear xxxx:

We are pleased to confirm your appointment as the importer for the following brands produced by Weber Wines exported to the United States of America, commencing 1st September, 2014:

Best Wines

Greatest Wines

Superb Wines

This appointment is effective for the following U.S. states:

New York

New Jersey

Maine

New Hampshire

Connecticut

Massachusetts

Should you have any questions regarding this appointment, please do not hesitate to contact the undersigned.

Yours sincerely,

Anika Weber
Managing Director
Weber Wines AG
Ph: +49 8888 8888

This second letter assigns U.S. exclusivity for all wines produced by the supplier:

(Winery letterhead)

Letter of Appointment as Exclusive Importer of Weber Wines into the USA

(date)

(importer's name and address)

Dear xxxx:

We are pleased to confirm your appointment as the exclusive importer for all wines produced by Weber Wines exported to the United States of America, commencing 1st September, 2014.

Should you have any questions regarding this appointment, please do not hesitate to contact the undersigned.

Yours sincerely,

Anika Weber
Managing Director
Weber Wines AG
Ph; +49 8888 8888

Here is a third alternative, particularly if you have had an importer prior to this appointment and wish to make it clear that this change has occurred. It is not necessary, but is an option you may prefer:

(Winery letterhead)

Letter of Appointment as Exclusive Importer of Weber Wines into the USA

(Date)

To Whom It May Concern:

Weber Wines is the owner and producer of the following brands:

(Brand Name/s)

Weber Wines hereby appoints (importer name) duly licensed by the Alcohol Tobacco Tax Bureau as exclusive Primary American Source and Importer of Record of the brands listed above for the United States (or for the following states) (itemize states if necessary to limit scope):

(states)

This appointment is effective immediately.

Where applicable, this appointment supersedes any previous appointments and/or agreements. All brand registrations, distributor appointments and price postings should be transferred to (Importer), for the above brands.

Should you have any questions regarding this appointment, please contact the undersigned. Thank you for your consideration.

Sincerely,

Anika Weber
Managing Director
Weber Wines AG
Ph: +49 8888 8888

I realize that to anyone outside the U.S., all requirements can feel daunting and somewhat forbidding. There is always the fear each time there is a registration, assignment, application or signing over of some rights, that this ties the winery/brand owner to some binding commitment from which they can never detach, or which will require money and legal representation to do so. *I will tell you when this might be the case.* I will also tell you when there is nothing to worry about and you can assign and register with impunity. The American Source Letter is the latter. This Appointment Letter, as it is sometimes called, is purely to state your intentions. It can be revised or revoked—by you—at any time. You may also designate several other importers as your representative through this vehicle. I would simply caution you not to take advantage of your importer, nor deceive them by assigning the same territory to multiple importers. It invites disaster. At best, you will create unnecessary work and expense for one or more of these importers, and the loss of potentially valuable distribution.

If revocation is required at any time, a letter of notice to the importer is sufficient if they are unaware of the change. No letter is actually required, but I think this is an appropriate way to bring closure to the arrangement. If there are to be territorial (state) reassignments, this should be discussed with the importer first to arrive at a satisfactory rearrangement, based on mutual understanding of the reasons, and to make sure there is no misinterpretation when a new importer starts selling in an area previously assigned to a former importer.

There is no need to notify anyone else, although the American Source letter to a subsequent importer might well include: "This letter supersedes all other assignments of territory to any other importer", or words to that affect, to demonstrate that a previous assignment is no longer valid. Including this paragraph will make it much easier and clearer for a new importer to register your brands in a state that requires the American Source letter.

COLA (Certificate of Label Approval)

Commitments made, wines chosen, now it is time for the process of applying to TTB for label approval to import these wines, known as COLA (Certificate of Label Approval). This is a role executed by your importer, or by a compliance company which is performing this function on behalf of your importer. This is a very complex subject to address in just one section, but some explanation should prepare you for what lies ahead. In brief, it is taking your own labels—front, back, neck strip, capsule, seal, button and whatever else you have on your wine bottle that contains wording— and reworking them so that they comply with U.S. regulations. In some instances, this requires a completely new set of labels. In others, an additional label is all that is necessary. Regardless, no wines can enter the U.S. for sale without an approved set of labels affixed to the bottle and a COLA.

The process of producing U.S. compliant labels seems to confound all wineries across the world, in my experience, whether or not English is their first language and whether or not they have previously exported to the U.S. So if you are confused by the U.S. label requirements, even after studying the information I will set forth in this book, you are not alone. Fortunately, most wine label printers are now familiar with the mandatory information and probably have a template. This was not the case when I began importing in 1992 and I painstakingly took every brand owner and/or printer through U.S. compliance line by line.

There are specific aspects to U.S. labels which must be adhered to without deviation, but if the printer follows these guidelines they will prepare a label graphic that should be submission-ready for you. That is not to say that the experienced printer will still not make mistakes and they often do. Omissions and misconceptions happen all the time, but once you learn what the basics are it is really very easy to review label proposals for compliance.

The basics for the mandatory information are these:

Brand Label
This can be a front or back label depending on where the mandatory information is in compliance:

1. Brand Name
2. Class or Type Designation (red table wine, for example or specific varietal, e.g. Zinfandel)
3. Percentage of blend (if applicable)
4. Appellation (if applicable)
5. Vintage (if applicable)

Any Label
This can be front, back or side:

1. Bottler's Name and Address
2. Alcohol Content
3. Net Contents (e.g.750ml)
4. Sulfite Declaration, specifically, "Contains Sulfites"
5. Health Warning Statement, as set out below:

GOVERNMENT WARNING: *(1) According to the Surgeon General, women should not drink alcoholic beverages during pregnancy because of the risk of birth defects. (2) Consumption of alcoholic beverages impairs your ability to drive a car or operate machinery, and may cause health problems.*

6. Importer Details: "Imported by..." and location (phone number and website optional)

There are minimum font sizes for the mandatory information and, dry as this may sound, becoming familiar with these requirements will also enable you to review and approve the printer's proofs like a pro. This information on font sizes is also directly from TTB:

Brand Name, Class/Type, Bottler's Name and Address, Net Contents, Sulfite Statement and Appellation

- At least 2 mm for containers larger than 187 ml
- At least 1 mm for containers 187 ml or less

Alcohol Content

- At least 1 mm but not larger than 3 mm for containers of less than 5 L

Health Warning Statement

- Not smaller than 3 mm for containers larger than 3 L with a maximum of 12 characters per inch
- Not smaller than 2 mm for containers over 237 ml to 3 L with a maximum of 25 characters per inch
- Not smaller than 1 mm for containers of 237 ml or less with a maximum of 40 characters per inch

The label graphics must be submitted to the importer via email in separate jpeg attachments, one each for all labels and separate seals, etc. There should be no surrounding or extraneous information, such as printer's marks, color notations or approval sign offs on design. Each label must be as it will look when printed and affixed to the bottle. Each attachment must be no more than 750kb.

There are three fairly recent changes to TTB's requirements I need to emphasize, because these will differ from my previous book, which was released prior to the changes. Most printers will be familiar with the changes, but others may not, so I have listed them here:

- Allowable jpeg attachment size increased from 450kb to 750kb
- TTB no longer checks actual size of font or label, although they retain the discretion to do so and require that you verify the size of each attachment
- Alc/vol or Alc by vol (the alcohol statement) is allowed on any label (front, back or side) effective August 9, 2013

Before we go any further, I will stress what I feel is one of the most important aspects of this particular issue: **under no circumstances should you print any of the labels until they are approved**, unless it is an exact duplicate of a previously approved label and the only thing to change is your unique importer details. Even the experienced printer and your importer's careful eye may miss a key element that will be the cause of label rejection.

According to TTB, here are the most common corrections needed.

Top Ten Submitter Corrections for COLAs Online

- The images that were submitted are illegible
- Images(s) were distorted during upload
- Dimensions provided generated a skewed or distorted image on the printable COLA
- Labels must be saved and uploaded as separate image files
- Files are uploaded in wrong area
- Problems with the Government Warning (Health Warning Statement)

    *They are very strict about the exact wording, punctuation, bold of the words "**Government Warning:**", but not the text itself*

- Terms are placed in incorrect field, e.g. "zinfandel" in the fanciful name field

    Example of fanciful name might be "Block 28 Reserve"

- Appellation of origin is missing from application

- You must designate a "brand (Front)" label
- Brand name on application does not match labels

These are examples of reasons for the TTB online application vehicle, COLAs Online, to return the application with a status of "needs correction." The "needs correction" notice is made immediately to the submitter and the resubmitted application receives priority attention. If all changes are not made when resubmitted or not made in a timeframe specified by TTB, the COLA will be rejected.

I will include a few additional items that are not permitted. They may not make the Top Ten on TTB's hit parade, but they are right up there when it comes to having your label rejected. Here are just a few of those I've personally experienced in labels sent to me for review, some of them very recently:

- "Fortified" is prohibited, even in a wine that has been fortified by grape spirit or brandy, suggesting that it has intoxicating characteristics and encourages drinking. Despite the fact that all wine has potentially intoxicating qualities this logic seems to elude TTB.
- Neither "intense" nor "powerful" can be used when referring to the wine; however, it is acceptable when referring to the palate or nose of the wine.
- No reference to a suggested standard drinks per bottle is allowed.
- Even descriptive text cannot refer to wines having "predominantly" a certain varietal, unless that varietal is listed in a way that imbues it with more significance and indicates a percentage, if it is less than 75%.
- The word "lively" cannot be applied to a still wine. This word signifies effervescence.
- The word "liqueur" cannot be used for a table wine, even when referring to a fortified dessert wine. It is a word reserved for distilled spirits.

Once a label is rejected, the wine will not be allowed to enter the country until a new submission is made from the beginning with the correct information. This submission must comply with the label on the bottle in the event of a customs inspection or individual state registrations. This is one reason, among the others stated above, why it makes sense to submit online. The average turnaround time (as of this writing) is around thirty days. It changes daily, varying as a result of label application volume, but TTB label scrutiny has been relaxed over the years, often resulting in a shorter timeframe despite the increased workload for TTB agents. Notification of either "needs correction" or "approved" will be made to your importer via email, who will then advise you.

For TTB's purposes, a "brand" label is considered the label on which the compliant information is recorded. If your front label omits the mandatory front label information, they would not consider this to be the "brand" label. An example is:

As you can see, there is no brand name on this label. Although it is affixed to the "front" of the bottle it cannot be considered the "brand" label.

On the other hand, the following would be considered the brand label (even though it is the back label) because it contains all the mandatory information:

```
                    ALLEGRETTI
                     VENETO
                    PROSECCO

   IMPORTED BY BLUESTONE WINE SOLUTIONS, CARLSBAD, CA, USA

   GOVERNMENT WARNING: (1) ACCORDING TO THE SURGEON GENERAL,
   WOMEN SHOULD NOT DRINK ALCOHOLIC BEVERAGES DURING
   PREGNANCY BECAUSE OF THE RISK OF BIRTH DEFECTS. (2)
   CONSUMPTION OF ALCOHOLIC BEVERAGES IMPAIRS YOUR ABILITY
   TO DRIVE A CAR OR OPERATE MACHINERY, AND MAY CAUSE
   HEALTH PROBLEMS. CONTAINS SULFITES

   BOTTLED BY PASQUALE ALLEGRETTI & SONS, VENETO, ITALY

   WINE OF ITALY    750ML           8% ALC/VOL
```

This is only a template and not meant to be construed as the only layout. A winery is free to choose graphics for their labels that look aesthetically pleasing and conform to their image, as long as all mandatory information is there in basically the order on the above label. Descriptive text could be inserted, so that it looks something like this, again, only an example:

Romeo Vin Santo is produced in small amounts from select parcels of the vineyard, a very special wine made from only the highest quality grapes, hand selected and laid to dry on lake reed mats for at least 120 days. Following a minimun five years of aging, the resulting Vin Santo in each small cask is unique. The wine is then bottle-aged. Romeo Vin Santo is ready only after ten or more years.

ROMEO
VIN SANTO DI MONTEPULCIANO 1993
Malvasia 60%, Pulcinculo 30%, Trebbiano 10%
DESSERT WINE - PRODUCT OF ITALY
IMPORTED BY BLUESTONE WINE SOLUTIONS, LLC CARLSBAD, CA, USA
GOVERNMENT WARNING: (1) ACCORDING TO THE SURGEON GENERAL, WOMEN SHOULD NOT DRINK ALCOHOLIC BEVERAGES DURING PREGNANCY BECAUSE OF THE RISK OF BIRTH DEFECTS. (2) CONSUMPTION OF ALCOHOLIC BEVERAGES IMPAIRS YOUR ABILITY TO DRIVE A CAR OR OPERATE MACHINERY, AND MAY CAUSE HEALTH PROBLEMS.
CONTAINS SULFITES   375 ml   ALC. BY VOL. 17.5%
ESTATE BOTTLED BY AZIENDA AGRICOLA ROMEO
Available in California through www.mikekaufherwines.com

In the above example, all mandatory statements are clear, including percentages of grapes. In addition, the label includes permitted descriptive text composed by the brand owner.

Although the above label was designed specifically for the U.S. market and could be distributed anywhere in the country, the label was intended solely for an online retailer for small batch wines. Therefore, certain details were not as critical as others. For example, there is no bar code on this back label. I suggest that a bar code is *essential* for any traditional wholesale distribution in the U.S. Most retail stores, large and small, will require it for cashier scanning and monitoring inventory. It is not worth taking the risk that your wines will only be in exclusive fine wine stores that do not scan barcodes, or in restaurants. There are too many variables and all other venues will not consider purchasing wines without the bar code.

An acceptable barcode in the U.S. is either the 12 digit UPC or 13 digit EAN. The U.S. agreed to accept the previously "European" bar code in 2005, but the EAN is now a UPC subset. If you have difficulty obtaining a bar code in your country, talk with your importer. An importer with some experience will have access to resources to provide a number. Although labels are normally the brand owner's responsibility, the importer can sometimes provide barcodes for your use, at their discretion.

Descriptive text is often a tiny portal into the vineyard and winemaking practices, philosophy and personalities of the brand owners. As such, it can be funny, flowery, evocative or informational (see Figure 11).

Many consumers do appreciate learning that the vineyard is planted on gravelly loam, that the wine was aged in French oak, or that the family is fifth generation. A suggested food pairing is also welcome. Just be aware that even descriptive text must conform to U.S. requirements to a degree. It cannot contain prohibited statements, be perceived to encourage drinking or contain offensive commentary. And if it is in a language other than English, TTB requires that your importer provide a translation. Of course, if

Figure 11   Brash Higgins Nero d'Avolo

your label is entirely in another language you have also somewhat limited your audience.

Purchase Orders

A purchase order from an importer is their commitment to you. It now goes beyond just a discussion and becomes a concrete intention (see Figure 12).

A purchase order is generated by the importer, but protects both parties in the specificity of its content. It should contain the following:

- Purchase order number (for tracking)
- Date
- Terms
- Price
- Payment currency
- Shipping point
- Vintage
- Consignor (the supplier, with contact details)
- Consignee (importer contact details, including licensed warehouse)
- Quantity
- Sample allowance (if applicable)

You should not deviate from whatever your importer has stipulated without prior notice and agreement. Imagine the importer is specifying a vintage that was especially good with this particular wine, a gold medal winner. Not only is the importer depending on this exact wine, but may well have pre-sold it, or produced marketing materials to announce its arrival. The importer orders it and receives the previous vintage. No gold medal, different taste and a tough sell. You may have thought they were aware that you would ship the vintage you were currently working through, not the gold medal winner you are releasing in two months. You may also have a difficult time selling this vintage domestically, but think it won't be a problem to move such a small quantity in the vast United States. Neither of these reasons should be part of your consideration at any time and your importer will not thank you for it.

You may be tempted to ship the remaining 150 cases of the previous Chardonnay vintage in stock and, since your order was for 250 cases, it

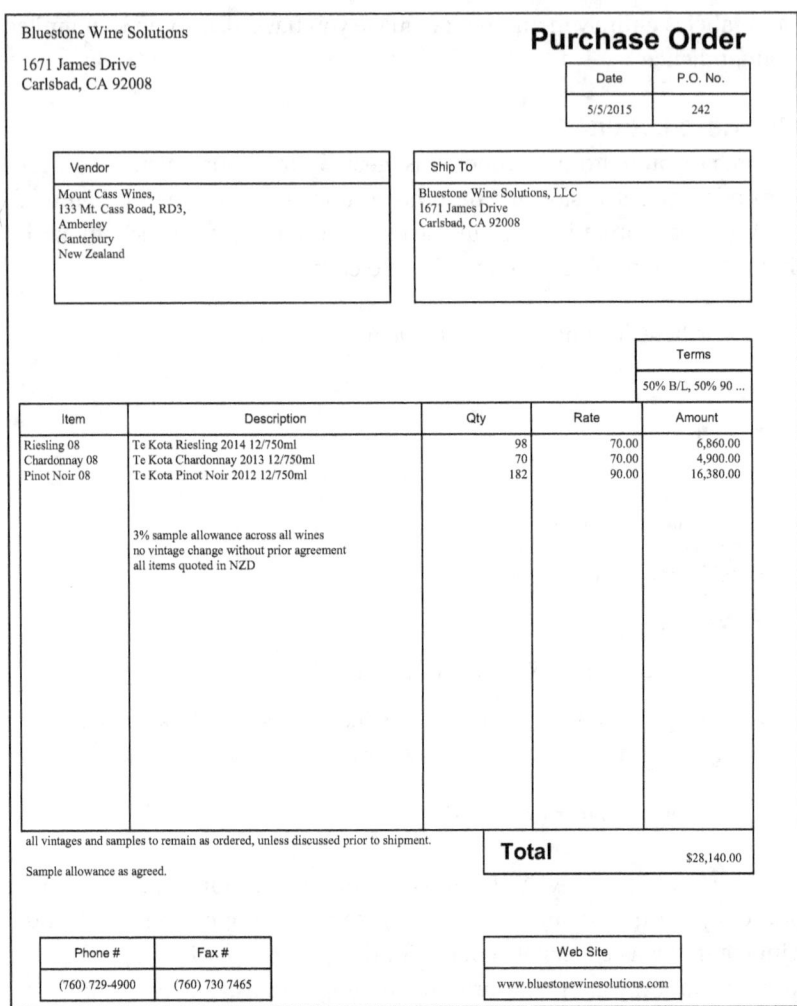

Figure 12 **Sample purchase order**

seems to make sense to deplete the previous vintage and make up the difference with the new. But now, instead of 250 cases of the current release, your importer has to list two different vintages on their price sheet, submit both to publications for review and presumably deal with the concern of having everyone choose the new over the old—U.S. tastes and expectations being what they are.

The exception to the above would be if you sold out of the anticipated vintage prior to the purchase order. That is entirely your prerogative, since you had nothing binding, but it is still something that should be discussed at the time of the purchase order and certainly prior to shipment. If the importer has not tasted the new vintage, you should send samples immediately. Vintage variation for estate-grown, smaller vineyards is the norm, rather than the exception. This does not mean it will be inferior of course; it may even be better. It gives your importer the opportunity to make their own assessment as to its perceived marketability and increase or reduce the order accordingly.

Marketing and POS Material

Website

These days most people have websites, but not all websites are created equal. In your case, is there an English translation? Does it have resources in the event a customer of your importer wants more information? All good importers will put together their own POS (Point of Sale) material for wholesale outreach or local retail calls, but it's often much easier and faster for a retail buyer to just go to a website when they want to promote the wine in their latest e-newsletter. Or for a restaurant that might want to educate their wait staff on a featured wine. Your website might previously have been a local tool for you in your country or designed for entirely different export markets. Or it may be a place card with a basic home page. But now you have U.S. representation and it is extremely helpful to provide history, new releases, wine descriptions, updates and bios on the winery or vineyard principals. The website can be dynamic or static, but it should provide current and practical guidance for browsers in idiomatic English. None of this is very difficult and it can always be handled by an IT resource, but either way an informative website is something relatively inexpensive that could be a great aid to your importer.

Brochures and Printed Background Materials

These are no longer that necessary in an age when materials can all be emailed in a Power Point slide presentation, zipped in an email folder, downloaded from the importer's website, or provided on a flash drive for the importer. Although, supplying the importer with a set of materials, if they are available, can always aid the importer's sales efforts. A professional set of materials, together with packaging, style, price and rapport with you, will build a foundation for the distributor and a desire to get behind the brand.

Tasting Notes

These are essential to your importer, but I realize that tasting notes, tech sheets, sell sheets or whatever one calls them are as different as winemakers themselves. Winemakers tend to compose notes in individual ways, sometimes as bare technical data and sometimes as a fluffy PR piece that would be interesting to a consumer at cellar door, but virtually useless to someone in the field. And what I have been provided with during my career has run the gamut from garbled dictation over the phone while the winemaker is weeding between rows of vines to glossy, full-color printed sheets packed with technical data, harvest highlights and comprehensive tasting notes. All of that, including viticulture and vinification is meaningful and valuable to your importer's efforts, but should ideally be kept to one sheet. Observations of the vineyard by the importer during a visit are equally important aspects in their marketing efforts. There is still no substitution for the mystique behind a wine's origins, the story of a family's founding of the vineyard, the beauty of a region and the presence of subjective influences such as terroir, biodynamics, irrigation or elevation.

A higher degree of technical data can be over-kill and a lesser degree amounts to a meaningless piece that no industry member appreciates. This is an actual example of *one of the latter*, currently in use by a U.S. importer. It says virtually nothing useful, except perhaps case production. It also originally contained numerous spelling errors, which I have corrected.

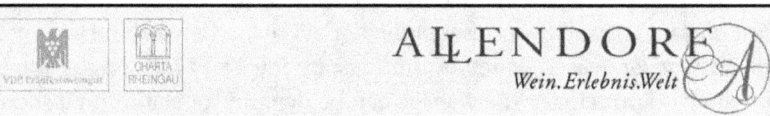

ALLENDORF RIESLING CLASSIC 2009
Rheingau, Germany

This standout winery was founded in 1773. They have a modern approach to winemaking with a focus rooted in the unique character of the region. The results are consistent, mineral rich wines with traditional flavors from the blue slate enriched soil.

In 2000 the German wine institute introduced two new denominations of Riesling; "Classic" and "Selection". The term Classic includes vintage wines from a region (in this case the Rheingau) that exemplifies the grape variety. The residual sugar content of the wine may be twice as high as its acid content, but no more than 15 grams. The intention of the classification is to reflect a wine of the category "grand-ordinaire". This style of wine will be off—dry.

12pk
Stainless steel fermentation
300 case production

2008 Chapel Hill McLaren Vale Cabernet Sauvignon

Winemakers Comments: The 2008 Chapel Hill Cabernet Sauvignon perfectly articulates the regional expression and charm of McLaren Vale. The close proximity of McLaren Vale to the Gulf of St Vincent and the resultant cooling afternoon sea breezes ensure that the grapes do not ripen too hastily and also facilitates the development of optimum levels of flavour, colour and tannin.

After a good start to the season, with soaking rains from April 07 through to July 07, a much drier period followed through to budburst in September. This meant an earlier than usual start to the growing season. After a hot start to January 2008, the temperature steadied resulting in ideal dry ripening conditions right through February. Daytime temperatures ranged from the mid-twenties to mid-thirties and night times remained cool.

The window of opportunity for Cabernet Sauvignon grapes to develop their optimum varietal flavour is very fine. Regular vineyard visits and tasting of the grapes is imperative to ensure that the grapes are not allowed to achieve over ripeness as this would diminish the varietal characters and result in undesirable non-descript "jammy" characters. The individual parcels of grapes were harvested separately and fermented on skins for a minimum of eight days. The ferments were managed to ensure a greater level of extraction earlier in ferment, with the ferment being handled more gently towards the end of the time on skins to ensure that any astringent or stalky tannins were not extracted.

The subsequent wine exudes an evocative array of flavours. Brooding mulberry, dark cherry, liquorice and roasted chestnut flavours all mingle harmoniously in the wine. The flavour profile is underpinned by the subtle and seamless integration of the spicy oak and the sumptuous finely grained tannin structure.

Variety: Cabernet Sauvignon
Appellation: 100% McLaren Vale
Harvest Date: Late February 2008 to early March 2008

Barrel Ageing: Matured for 19 months in 300 L oak hogsheads, of which 91% was French and 9% American. Oak age was 32% new, 35% second use and 33% third use
Acidity: 6.9 g/L
pH: 3.52
Alcohol: 14.5 % v/v
Residual Sugar: 2.2 g/L
Bottled: 11th November 2009
Released: March 2010
Winemaker: Michael Fragos and Bryn Richards

Please remember that I said the Allendorf tasting note is *not* recommended. It appears to be saying something without actually saying much at all. Certainly, it says nothing specific about the wine.

Conversely, for me, the *2008 Chapel Hill McLaren Vale Cabernet Sauvignon* is a great tasting note. It provides salient points regarding viticulture and vinification, without getting too technical, along with more interesting background details that paint a picture for the customer, along with a photo of the bottle. If the customer wants more detail, they or the importer can always contact you.

I find the following details to be helpful, for which I have included one type of example for each. These are only examples. There are many other ways that the more subjective areas can be characterized and described and much of the information would be grouped in sections:

1. Synopsis of conditions for that vintage, including anything that made it particularly difficult or particularly favorable

    The climate is characterized by hot summer days and relatively cool nights with diurnal ranges of up to 26 degrees Celsius. The 2002 season was an exceptional vintage, long and warm with cool nights, which is reflected in the wine. The summer/autumn rainfall was low.

2. When grapes were picked and how

    Grapes were harvested by hand. Each clone of fruit was harvested separately and kept separate at all stages of vinification. The fruit was de-stemmed, with some batches having a percentage of whole clusters retained.

3. Yield

    The vineyard is trellised on a Geneva double curtain and spur pruned to 10 shoots per meter. It is extensively thinned to 6 tonnes per hectare.

4. Varietal, including percentages of blended grapes, no matter how small—the purpose being to identify what is in the wine, not to comply with a legal requirement

    Cabernet Sauvignon 72%, Merlot 23%, Petit Verdot 5%

5. Where grown (estate, sourced, or some description, for example)

    Soils are free-draining river gravels.

6. Fermentation process

   The must then underwent 3–5 days of pre-ferment maceration after which it was warmed to 17 degrees and inoculated for fermentation. Most batches were pressed off at dryness while some were left on skins for 7–8 days.

7. Aging, including type of oak if oak aged

   14 months in seasoned French oak.

8. Other details of interest, such as whether it was fined and filtered, whether the grapes were organically or biodynamically grown, etc.

   Sourced from 90-year-old bush grown vines in the northeast of the valley. All fruit was organically grown on the estate and certified by NOP (National Organic Program).

9. Description of wine characteristics such as color, weight, flavors, finish—this is a very subjective area that becomes a bow to the winemaker's own style, which can be short and succinct or flowery hyperbole

   Color: *Intense garnet.*

   Aroma: *Lifted perfume of rose petals, cedar and cigar box with hints of spearmint, overlaying a heady blend of cinnamon, nutmeg and brown cardamom.*

   Palate: *A complex array of pungent herbs leading into a fleshy mid-palate of blackcurrant and black cherries. The wine is superbly finished by elegant, structural grape tannins and balanced with subtle integrated oak.*

10. Technical data, such as that which relates to a particular wine

Sulfur dioxide at bottling—Total (ppm)	42
pH	3.40
Acid (g/L)	6.80
C6 Sugars (g/L)	0
Alcohol (%)	13.9

11. If relevant, ratings and internationally recognized awards. Do not clutter up the sheet with extraneous details of obscure medals or less than impressive results.

    94 Points—Wine Spectator (make sure it is for the current vintage)
    Gold Medal—San Francisco Wine Competition
    Decanter—Top 100 Wines of 2014

12. Food pairing suggestions, which are at the discretion of the wine-maker—not essential by any means, but often an interesting guide

    Serve with grilled meat and mature Saint-Marcellin cheese.

This is a lengthy list, but as you can see, some aspects can be handled in a word or number. Ultimately, the more comprehensive it can be, the more you have equipped your importer to discuss the wines in an informed and knowledgeable fashion. A tasting note/tech sheet can be in many different styles, but none of that is important (beyond being neat and clear) as long as it includes much or all of the essential information. You will no doubt have your own style that will bring a sense of individuality and the right impression for your wines.

Shelf Talkers

These are those small cards that hang from the shelf in front of a bottle in a retail store. They are normally prepared by your importer, either as a printed set of cards, or more often these days, uploaded to a trade section of the importer's website for access by distributors or retailers to print their own. They should be oriented to the American consumer and, when possible, include a high rating from a recognized U.S. publication. If there is no review or rating, a good shelf talker should provide an appealing taste profile for the consumer. Not all stores will allow shelf talkers, but in those that do, a shelf talker puts your wine on equal footing with all the wines vying for attention, or hopefully makes it stand out. Figures 13 and 14 show a couple of examples of shelf talkers with and without ratings.

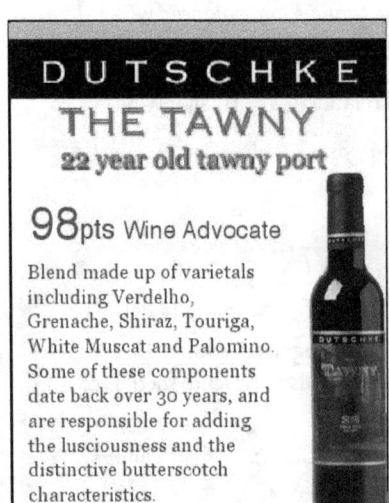

Figure 13   Shelf talker with rating   *Figure 14*   Shelf talker without rating

Case Cards

These are for use in retail stores to display wines in a 12-bottle case. This is usually customary when a retailer has made a volume purchase of three or more cases for a "case stack". The case card can be specific to the actual wine for the following reasons:

- There is only one wine sold to the U.S. under this brand
- The review, rating or demand for one wine is so high that focusing on the singular wine directs store traffic to the cases
- The winery's budget permits multiple case cards for each wine

More commonly, the case card is non-specific, displaying an eye-catching graphic for the brand for any wine in its portfolio. Case cards are the width of a side of a wine box and slotted to fit in the box to stand upright. Figures 15 and 16 are examples of specific and nonspecific case cards.

* * *

Figure 15 Specific case card   *Figure 16* Nonspecific case card

Final Thoughts

Don't underestimate the power of marketing, for both practical benefits and general customer goodwill. I knew a state distributor who decided to become an importer, concluding that if he could distribute wines he imported, he extended his reach by selling to other states and exert further control over the wines as both importer and distributor in his own state. There was nothing wrong with this reasoning, except that he continued to think like a state wholesaler. He had been a distributor for so long that he failed to realize that an importer must operate from a greater distance and provide sufficient tools to his distributors for them to be an extension of the company. His technical sheets on wine are non-existent and his tasting notes are virtually useless. For years he had been telling his own sales staff not to worry about "the technical stuff" and "just tell them the wine is good", which meant they had to find creative ways to sell the wine, sometimes through pricing and sometimes through their own research to cobble together sufficient information to satisfy their customers. To instruct his own state salespeople in this way may or may not have worked for him. To tell unconnected distributors in other states the same thing was not the way to establish or develop a collaborative relationship, and it cost him business. This is not what you want your importer doing. You want them as invested in this process as you are and almost as knowledgeable about the wine's journey from vineyard to table.

9

Logistics

Although there are many different countries and ports from which to export to the U.S., and therefore variations on the following advice and suggestions, the basis for logistical considerations is the same. Some logistics will be handled by you, the wine supplier, and some by your purchaser, the importer. In each situation, which of these becomes your responsibility will be agreed upon between the two of you. Whilst there are conventional arrangements in the U.S., which I'll draw attention to as we come to them, there are no hard and fast rules. Ultimately, it's about financial and scheduling benefits:

- How to ship
- Who to ship with (freight company)
- Whether to use a freight forwarder
- Consolidations or full containers
- Who is paying for shipping
- When the ship needs to leave and arrive
- Whether other wineries from your area are involved

First of all, let's consider payment. Different payment options will affect your price and your level of control and responsibility.

Payment Terms

Incoterms (International Carrier Terms)

Incoterms are commercial terms widely used in the shipping industry. Although you will find that the most common form of payment arrangements are generally FOB (Free on Board) and EXW (ex-works), it is still worthwhile to be familiar with the term CIF (Cost, Insurance and Freight) in the event you would like to offer it as an alternative, or it has been requested by the importer, and generally to educate yourself as to the difference.

> **CIF** means that the exporter (you) arranges and pays for the vessel and insures the freight during the voyage. The winery, or your export agent, also arranges all shipping details, including selection of the vessel, consolidation and packing of the goods and monitoring of the shipment. This could include direct contact with the steamship company or a freight forwarder. You may enjoy the control aspect of this arrangement, or you may feel that it affords you additional economies of scale for other export opportunities by giving all your business to one shipping company.
>
> Legal and financial responsibility passes to the importer when the wine arrives at the destination dock. This means the importer can minimize their initial financial outlay and is not responsible for making the logistical arrangements for a container. This can be an advantage to them at the initial stage when they may be unfamiliar with the process or the foreign country. Despite this, an importer will not often opt for CIF, since they are eventually paying for these costs through your wine price. Additionally, the importer will be aware that you or the export agent will presumably add some markup for this responsibility, and the importer gives up control of their own shipment. If you are dealing with a first-time importer where startup finances are a consideration for them and you see this as good investment in your relationship, then CIF may be an attractive option for both of you.
>
> **FOB** is an often misunderstood term. The original definition for FOB meant title passed "at the ship's rail" and originated during the time of sailing ships when goods were actually passed by hand over the rail of the ship. Since containerization, and particularly in the U.S., FOB is characteristically understood to mean from "port of origin" so that title for the goods passes to the importer when they are delivered to the origination shipping port. Depending upon your

understanding with the importer, it can also mean FOB winery or whatever point the seller releases goods to the buyer, but strictly speaking this term would be known as FCA (Free Carrier - named place). In other words, where the seller designates is the point of pickup. It is important to make sure both you and the importer have the same definition for this term. In any FOB scenario in the U.S. wine industry, the importer is responsible for all duty, taxes, customs clearance and overland freight at destination, and in this case they are also responsible for securing and paying for ocean freight and insurance. This is the most common financial term, because it allows the importer to choose their own shipping company, develop their own relationship with a freight forwarder or consolidator, make their own bookings to suit their time constraints or planned arrivals and be informed of any delays or problems en route. Most importers would also want to ensure that they are responsible for negotiating what they may assume will be more competitive shipping rates and establish a direct relationship with their own freight forwarder.

EXW is also called ex-cellars by some in reference to wine, but means the same thing. The supplier makes the wine available at the vineyard or winery. This arrangement places the maximum financial and logistical obligation on the importer, but may make sense where you do not have the means to transport the wine and where the importer may wish to take control of arranging a coordinated pickup of several pallets from different wineries or vineyards. EXW also means that the importer incurs the risks for bringing the goods to their final destination, so be sure this is clearly understood by both parties.

You are also free to develop your own agreement with the importer. You may agree to share the costs, and therefore the profits, or provide discounts or surcharges for certain arrangements. It's all in the understanding you have, although it essentially depends upon the sensitive price points that may be adversely or positively affected.

Shipping Terminology and Regulations

Whether or not you are the one arranging the shipment, it is helpful to understand some of the terminology, especially if you have not encountered it before. And some of it is relevant only to the U.S.

Sizes and Weights

All cargo shipments coming into a U.S. port must also move overland and therefore come under road laws governed by both federal and local government weight restrictions. There are two sizes for containers, referred to as 20 foot and 40 foot. Whilst you would think you can cram more into a 40 foot container, this is not actually so. A 20 foot container weight is limited to 39,500 lbs and a 40 foot container to 44,500 lbs. Although there are state variations that allow one to exceed the weight limits, with the use of special equipment to distribute chassis weight more equitably on roads and bridges, it hardly seems worth the effort, cost and risk. The consequences of exceeding the legal limit are fines, rejection of load and potential damage, and having to offload the contents into other transportation.

In addition, Long Beach, a common West Coast port, has its own restrictions, which are:

- 20' (general purpose) in excess of 44,000 cargo weight lbs
- 20' (reefer) in excess of 41,500 cargo weight lbs
- 40' (general purpose) in excess of 44,500 cargo weight lbs
- 40' (reefer) in excess of 41,500 cargo weight lbs
- 45' in excess of 41,500 cargo weight lbs

Depending upon whether your wines are palletized (on pallets) or stuffed (loaded without pallets), the capacity of a 20 foot container averages 700 to 1100 cases, based on 9 liter cases (12 × 750ml bottles). Importers' options may be influenced by several factors in their choice, including demand for the wines (that is if a large order has been placed and there is some urgency to fill it) and the cost of unloading it at the other end. Trucking companies and warehouses will spend more time unloading unpalletized wine and will charge the importer accordingly.

Pallets
A pallet, also known as a skid, is a flat, wooden structure with slats, used to confine the cases in a (usually) shrink wrapped, stacked configuration, with access underneath for a forklift to raise and move the load around with stability. Typically, the average U.S. pallet is deemed to hold 56 cases. In other parts of the world the pallet load is considered to be anywhere between 50 and 70 cases, so this is also a fact to keep in mind when discussing pallets with your importer. You may both be talking about different amounts when you refer to an order as "five pallets".

Final palletizing of your wine for an ocean freight container may depend upon load distribution and may not adhere to a generally accepted number of cases or layers. In discussion with people in the U.S., once again keep in mind that each of you may have a different number in mind when referring to a pallet, or pallet order as it relates to logically filling a container.

U.S. Customs and Border Protection, a department of Homeland Security, enacted regulations in 2004, which were enforced in its final form in 2006, to reduce the incidence of transported plant pests into the U.S. As a result of this ruling, all pallets (which come under the heading of Wood Packing Materials or WPM) must be treated and stamped with a mark certifying that the heat treatment or fumigation has been undertaken according to prescribed guidelines. More information can be found on their website www.cbp.gov. The ruling has been in place long enough now that all freight forwarders, agents, ports and shipping companies will be familiar with the requirements, but this is just one of those checklist items that is easy to confirm at the outset and disastrous if it is discovered to have been overlooked at a critical juncture.

Wood Packing Materials
It is imperative that all wood packing in your shipment, whether it is pallets, crating, special packaging of your wine or additional products accompanying the wines, meet U.S. federal regulations. These are no longer guidelines but are fully in force. I have paraphrased and abbreviated for clarity in certain places, but essentially, according to the USDA (United States Department of Agriculture) APHIS portal (Animal and Plant Health Inspection Service), a Final Rule for new requirements concerning the importation of WPM was published on September 16, 2004. The implementation date for regulatory enforcement began on September 16, 2005. There was a further ten months (July 5, 2006) until actual implementation, to allow countries to comply with International Standards for Phytosanitary Measures (ISPM 15) and the Final Rule. Failure to meet these standards will result in rejection of WPM in cargo shipments at U.S. ports of entry due to noncompliance with the ISPM 15 Standard. The link to this ruling is here: www.aphis.usda.gov/import_export/plants/plant_imports/wood_packaging_materials.shtml This rule states that all regulated WPM must be appropriately treated and marked under an official program developed and overseen by the National Plant Protection Organization (NPPO) in the country of export. All regulated WPM must be appropriately treated and marked under an official program developed and overseen by the NPPO in the country of export. The rule further states that any discovery of certain pests and insects signifies that the wood was not properly treated in accordance with standards and will not be allowed into the United States.

Reefer vs. Dry vs. Blanket vs. Insulated

Choice of container type will depend upon pragmatic business decisions—cost, time of year and availability. At no time do I recommend a dry container with no protection, but I give you the options as they exist.

> **Reefers** are refrigerated containers that control the temperature for the contents of the container, via a generator, for the duration of the voyage. It adds cost to ocean freight, but guarantees that the goods will arrive in optimum condition. That said, there is a difference between a reefer and a "working" reefer. In the latter this means that the generator is turned on. A "non-working" reefer is insulated, but not refrigerated. Your specific choice should be made clear at the time of booking.
>
> **Insulated** or thermal containers provide insulation on all sides of the box, but no refrigeration unit.
>
> **Thermal** blankets can be requested from your shipping company to provide insulation for the wine at an affordable cost. Liners have improved over the years to the extent that they have replaced thermal blankets as an economical but much more effective protection against heat and humidity.
>
> **Dry** containers are not temperature controlled. They are metal boxes in which the wine is either palletized or stuffed, and temperatures can fluctuate dramatically during the ocean voyage.

An insulated container can be sufficient during temperate months, especially from the same hemisphere, where the wine is not passing from summer to winter or vice versa, but this will most likely not be sufficient in summer and should not be risked. Just remember, in opting for a reefer, it will negate its benefits for your importer if you do not also concern yourself with temperatures during overland transport to port, the conditions during consolidation at port and the temperature of a port warehouse during waiting time. I have heard of many instances of unprotected cases of wine baking on a dock or in a stifling warehouse prior to shipment.

Freight Forwarder

It can be very worthwhile to engage a freight forwarder to arrange shipping through a volume contract with freight companies. With their specialized expertise, a freight forwarder is able to negotiate rates, determine shipping line schedules, book ships, coordinate shipments from multiple suppliers and keep you and the importer informed during the consolidation and pre-boarding stages. They are provided with a purchase order, which apprises them of the exact goods to expect for the shipment. They can help arrange pickup, do an inventory upon receipt at port and notify appropriate parties whether wines match the P.O or are damaged. They are the contact point for suppliers at the country of origin, which makes it easier for the importer, a continent away. A freight forwarder can avoid delays by staying on top of all export paperwork requirements from the country of origin and any other needs of the shipping line. They should be proactive in contacting you or the importer if they know there is some urgency to the shipment by, for example, finding an earlier booking date.

Consolidations

Consolidating product can be something your importer does to bring in a collection of imported wines from one region or country to make up a Full Container Load (FCL). Another type of consolidation is through a commercial carrier with multiple, unrelated shippers called a Less than Container Load (LCL), appropriate when your importer does not have sufficient cases in an order to fill a container, or prefers smaller, more frequent orders until they have built up some volume. An FCL minimum is around 500 cases, meaning that it becomes economical to contract for an entire container at this point. Although, even as few as 400 cases should be weighed against the cost of the LCL convenience. Freight is charged by what can fit in the vessel, whether it is a 20 foot or 40 foot container. Generally, the more you can put in it, the less it costs per case to ship. However, financial consideration go beyond that for any importer, who may then have a considerable amount of wine accumulating storage charges at their destination warehouse in the States, or may not need more than 300 cases, for example, for their immediate needs. In these instances, a consolidation, although more expensive per case for freight, becomes a practical option.

In the case of a consolidation in the importer's own container, that is, shipping your wines along with the importer's other wines in a container contracted by the importer, this will be viewed as an FCL and charged accordingly by the shipping line.

In either case, coordination is a factor in the overall logistics and you must be ready to meet the time constraints of either the independent commercial carrier or the importer's own shipment. That means adhering to a timeline that includes sufficient notice for bottling, labeling, boxing and transporting wine to the consolidation point. Depending on the country, a freight forwarder can arrange for the pickup of goods from your own winery or vineyard, but it will come at a price, and might be en route to others in the area at a time that is not convenient to you. This may be your only option, but sometimes it is more cost-effective for you to ensure that the wine is brought to the port yourself. Any winery that is not ready will have to be left behind until the next shipment, a potentially catastrophic consequence for both you and the importer.

Prior Notice
In addition to the FDA registration process you completed either before you shipped samples or appointed an importer, the second phase of the regulations require a "prior notice" for all shipments entering the U.S. Your importer must formally advise FDA of shipments bound for the U.S. prior to their arrival, most usually through their customs broker. Prior notice precedes customs entry and contains information retrieved from the shipping documents (commercial invoice and bill of lading) including the registration number(s) of the relative foreign facilities.

Prior notice is required for all food products entering the U.S. regardless of quantity and includes wine, beer and spirits samples, and it must be submitted no earlier than 5 days before estimated arrival of the product and no later than:

- 2 hours before arrival by land by road
- 4 hours before arrival by air or by land by rail
- 8 hours before arrival by water.

After submission of Prior Notice, your importer will receive a confirmation number, confirming that FDA has received the notification. Please be aware that any "food product" that arrives in port without having received this Prior Notice confirmation can be refused entry into the U.S. Where Prior Notice has been omitted, the shipment will sit in U.S. Customs holding until it is completed and submitted. If time is exceeded (usually 7 days), Customs has the option to return the wine or start charging costly demurrage if it stays, payable by the importer to U.S. Customs before release.

Invoice, Packing Slip, Bill of Lading
There are several documents that will need to be provided to a freight forwarder who will share these with the importer's customs broker and the importer. Of these, you will provide a commercial invoice and a packing slip. The invoice can also serve as a packing slip if it includes all information required on both documents.

Commercial Invoice

A commercial invoice is a document used in foreign trade. It acts as a customs declaration provided by the person or corporation that is exporting an item across international borders. Although there is no standard format, the document must include some specific information, such as the parties involved in the shipping transaction, the goods being transported, the country of manufacture and the Harmonized System codes for those goods. A commercial invoice must also include a statement certifying that the invoice is true, and a signature.

Packing List

The packing list (also known as a bill of parcel, unpacking note, packaging slip, (delivery) docket, delivery list, manifest, customer receipt or shipping list) is a document that details the contents, and often dimensions and weight, of each package or container. It informs all parties involved with shipping, including transport agencies, government authorities, and customers, about the contents of the package. It helps the parties deal with the package accordingly.

In the case of wine, the packing list is usually the tax invoice issued by the winery. Because it also itemizes the wine types, number of units, price, currency, terms and some shipping details, it takes the place of an additional packing slip.

Figure 17 shows one such example of a document layout, although there is no set format as long as the relevant information is included.

Bill of Lading

The Bill of Lading (B/L) is the document that covers transport by sea. Signed by the carrier, whether a shipping line or a freight forwarder, the B/L serves as a receipt to the consignor for the goods, as evidence of the contract of transport containing the conditions of transport, and as a document of title by which possession of the goods can be transferred. Typically, a B/L is issued in a set of three signed originals (or negotiables), one of which must be presented to claim the goods upon which the others become void. However, most B/Ls are Express and therefore called Non Negotiable, explained further below.

A bill of lading includes the following:

- Shipper name and address
- Consignee name and address

- Notify Party name and address
- Carrier Information
- Place of Departure
- Port of Loading
- Destination
- Cargo information—cargo description, weight, etc.
- Classification of the commodity

	(Name and Address of Winery)						
Date							
		TAX INVOICE					
(To Whom Sold – i.e. importer)							
Item Code Description		Qty	Unit	Pric	Disc	Currency	Total
(winery code) (wine details)		672	bottles	3.25	0	Euro	2184
(winery code) (wine details)		672	bottles	3.25	0	Euro	2184
						Total:	4368
Delivery Address:	Payment Terms:						
Bank details (for a wire transfer from your importer, if applicable):							
Signature of consignees:							

Figure 17 **Packing list**

Non-Negotiable Bill of Lading

A non-negotiable B/L (see Figure 18) declares that the cargo is consigned to a specific person and is Non Negotiable. If the carrier or someone else holds a lien over the transported cargo, the goods will not be released until that debt is paid. The endorsee is obligated by the lien.

Express Release—Sea Waybill

A Sea Waybill Express Release of ocean freight shipment means that no Bill of Lading originals are required in order to claim possession of the cargo at destination. The ocean freight can be claimed with only a copy of the B/L received by email or fax. A Sea Waybill Express Release is issued upon full payment of the ocean freight. This is the customary, and preferable, option to clear cargo at sea and, barring any unforeseen delays by customs, allows

Date:

NON-NEGOTIABLE

WAYBILL NUMBER:

SHIPPER	
Name: Address: City/State/Zip: FOB: ☐	VOYAGE NUMBER: PORT OF LOADING: OCEAN VESSEL:
CONSIGNEE	
Name: Location #: ________ Address: City/State/Zip: FOB: ☐	CARRIER: OCEAN VESSEL:
NOTIFY PARTY	
Name: Address: City/State/Zip:	PORT OF DISCHARGE ________________ Freight Charge Terms: Prepaid _____ Collect _____ 3rd Party _____
SPECIAL INSTRUCTIONS:	☐ (check box) Master Bill of Lading: with attached underlying Bills of Lading (if applicable)

PRE CARRIAGE BY	PLACE OF RECEIPT	FINAL DELIVERY:

CARRIER INFORMATION

MARKS AND NOS / CONTAINER SEALS	NO AND KIND OF PACKAGES	GROSS CARGO WEIGHT	TARE	DESCRIPTION OF PACKAGES AND GOODS AS STATED BY SHIPPER SHIPPERS LOAD STOW AND COUNT	MEASUREMENT

Weight in Kgs, Total (1) container:
ABOVE PARTICULARS DECLARED BY SHIPPER. CARRIER NOT RESPONSIBLE

Where the rate is dependent on value, shippers are required to state specifically in writing the agreed or declared value of the property as follows:
"The agreed or declared value of the property is specifically stated by the shipper to be not exceeding ____________ per ____________."

Amount: $ ________________
Fee Terms: Collect: ☐ Delivery: ☐ FOB: ☐

NOTE Liability Limitation for loss or damage in this shipment may be applicable.

RECEIVED, subject to individually determined rates or contracts that have been agreed upon in writing between the carrier and shipper, if applicable, otherwise to the rates, classifications and rules that have been established by the carrier and are available to the shipper, on request, and to all applicable state and federal regulations.

The carrier shall not make delivery of this shipment without payment of freight and all other lawful charges.
________________________ Shipper Signature

SHIPPER SIGNATURE / DATE
This is to certify that the above named materials are properly classified, described, packaged, marked and labeled, and are in proper condition for transportation
____

Loaded: ☐ By Shipper
Freight Counted: ☐ By Shipper

CARRIER SIGNATURE / PICKUP DATE
Carrier acknowledges receipt of packages and required placards. Carrier certifies emergency response information was made available and/or carrier has the U.S. DOT emergency response guidebook or equivalent documentation in the vehicle.
Property described above is received in good order, except as noted
________________________.

Figure 18 Non-Negotiable Bill of Lading

your importer to take possession faster with a smooth transition from port to warehouse.

* * *

Final Thoughts

If you don't become familiar with common wine industry terms and logistical arrangements then this could end up costing you thousands of dollars or result in unnecessary confusion between you and your importer. Issues such as approved wood pallets and FDA compliance are components of U.S. mandatory requirements. Making the wrong decision on the former or forgetting the latter will result in delays and potential rejection of the shipment.

Many items related to wine logistics in the U.S. become the responsibility of the importer, but it is always in your best interests to understand both your rights and your responsibilities. Knowledge will also allow you to negotiate pricing and contracts from an informed position and establish your role from the outset.

10

A Meeting of the Minds

At some point, there will be a different discussion about pricing and positioning. It will evolve from the abstract to the concrete, from the general to the particular. You have already found and vetted the importer and established you can work together. This is a huge achievement and its significance in this new endeavor cannot be underestimated. However, there will most likely come a time when you have definite ideas about your product and the importer has others. Let's explore some of these ideas and where compromise may be possible, or where the will of one or the other should prevail, to the benefit of the enterprise and your relationship.

Pricing—In Depth

You have already given your prices to your new U.S. partner. This is your price from the winery or port, at which point the importer takes possession. You may have arrived at that price via a somewhat arbitrary route, perhaps looking at your neighbor's wines and deciding you should price yours accordingly. Or slightly less. Or a lot more. Pricing is often a subjective decision, based on perception and nothing more. Do you think your wines are better than your neighbor's? Does your neighbor's wine sell? Is their soil type, irrigation, age of vines, time in oak, cost of oak, aging, bottles and labels the same? Most likely not.

You may be someone who is aware of every expense in the final product from growing the grapes, making the wine, bottling, packaging and overhead. From this you formulate your price to the buyer, with whatever margin you feel is necessary to your venture. If that is the case, then there is probably not a great deal of discussion or compromise necessary. This is the price that allows you to support your business and its continued viability and there is nothing wrong with this decision.

Remember, the price you charge visitors to your cellar door, or at the local tasting room in your village, is not the price you will quote the importer. You may be accustomed to a steady stream of customers in your local area, but now that you have decided to take this to a new business level, it is necessary to consider a wholesale price designed to attract an international sales volume and calculated and supported accordingly.

Looking at it from a QPR ratio (which your importer surely will do), does the price of your wine reflect greater perceived value? Have you done market research for comparable wines from your region in the U.S.? If there is no comparable area, with what could you compare your Tempranillo or Cabernet Sauvignon? If it tastes like a Rioja Tempranillo or a Napa Cabernet Sauvignon does your wine represent much better value? Because an unknown brand from an unfamiliar region will have to over-deliver to penetrate the market, no matter how good it is.

This pricing discussion may be initiated by the importer if he or she feels there is insufficient evidence to support the pricing, or has had an opportunity to taste the wines with others and there is a consensus that the wines should be introduced at a lower price point. Is this feasible for you? Have you calculated your costs so that you know what margin you can afford to give up, if any? A pricing discussion should not be motivated by an importer trying to secure your wines for a pittance, just because they want to sell them more easily, or make a larger profit themselves. It should be a conversation that involves an understanding of how the importer arrived at this conclusion, whether you can support it and whether a compromise is possible.

The ultimate goal, for both of you, is of course to sell wine. Be open to the prospect that your importer is more experienced in these matters and has a reason for suggesting a lower price, if that is the case. The issue with dropping the price too far is that you cannot expect to raise it significantly once the brand is established. There will be a revolt among those who have bought the wine—distributor and retailer—and taken considerable time to establish it at a certain level. The resistance will most likely extend to dropping the brand and that is the end of sales.

Personally, I don't believe a large, arbitrary price increase is ever justified, although there are those who will use justification in the form of accolades, ratings and demand. I believe there is an implicit contract with the consumer not to play games with a wine's price. A wine a customer may have bought and loved at a certain price, could be quickly priced out of reach or no longer considered reasonable value merely because of a high rating. Exchange rates, increasing production costs, poor harvest resulting in much higher quality, are all reasons to increase pricing, but this normally follows some historical demand for an established brand.

Some brand owners have difficulty understanding why their wine is priced so high once it gets into the American consumer's hands. They often think that the importer's margin must be much higher than it should be. Although they may grasp the concept of a three-tier system in the U.S., truly appreciating that each of these tiers is taking their own piece of the wine price pie can be another matter. I broached the subject of the three-tier system for alcohol regulation in the chapter on misconceptions, but I find that even when I think I have made a clear, detailed explanation, and saying more will feel redundant, comprehension often remains elusive because it is a system that is so alien to the way the rest of the world operates.

Many a discussion with a producer will begin with their assumption that the wine will sell for a figure they have in their head, without regard to the way the U.S. operates. It is not uncommon for a brand owner to say to the importer something like, "If you buy the wine from me at €12, then you will be able to sell it for €20."

So, if you are still confused, because none of the rest of the world operates in this way, you are not alone. First of all, the three-tier method of wine distribution has been controversial. It remains largely the bastion of giant distributors, who protect their significant proportion of wine and beer sales in their state through maintaining the three-tier system. To that end, they will often lobby congress to keep laws in place and are vociferous opponents of any attempts to erode legislation. On the website of a beer wholesale membership association, I read the simple statement, "The 3-Tier System: It's What Works". Clearly, as an entity representing beer distributors in this state, they are heavily invested in protecting their position. Organizations such as this have the following perspective on the three-tier laws:

- Each tier has separate ownership and operates independently. The three-tier system was designed to keep manufacturers, distributors, and retailers distinct and independent from one another.

- The three-tier system ensures that alcohol is not sold to minors nor sold or delivered through improper, unlawful channels.
- The three-tier system protects the economy because licensed distributors act in cooperation with the federal and state governments to help ensure that alcoholic beverage taxes are reliably collected.

All of this is true and these are valid reasons to maintain a discrete structure for alcohol sales, but in country as large, diverse and fragmented as the U.S., with its fifty states and fifty independently operating seats of government, this can be unwieldy and attach an undue burden to wineries, smaller importers, retailers and ultimately the consumer.

It is essential to remember that no matter who contacts you with interest in your wines, no matter how enthusiastic, they cannot do anything to facilitate the export/import, sale and distribution of your products without an importer. Later in the book we will explore some alternative ways to penetrate the market that may be available to you, but none of it *replaces* or circumvents the aforementioned system. We can just be creative about utilizing options that generate opportunity.

The table serves as an illustration of what the margins can be throughout the three tiers and how FOB ends up at retail. These formulas are by no means an absolute. Each entity in the system has the prerogative to build their own margins, based on whatever criteria they wish. In addition, freight and taxes vary from state to state, and can impact the price significantly. However, there are some general guidelines that can be used to narrow down the retail price range, and perhaps explain how the wine sells for so much more once it gets into the consumer's hands.

Column A	Column B	Column C	Column D	Column E	Column F	Column G
Bottle (USD)	Case (12 btl)	Clearance at $12 (USD)	Imp mrkup (FOB) x1.35	Wholesale x1.45	Retail/ cs (store) x1.5	Retail/ bottle
$2.00	$24.00	$36.00	$48.60	$70.47	$105.71	$8.81
$2.50	$30.00	$42.00	$56.70	$82.22	$123.32	$10.28
$3.00	$36.00	$48.00	$64.80	$93.96	$140.94	$11.75
$3.50	$42.00	$54.00	$72.90	$105.71	$158.56	$13.21
$4.00	$48.00	$60.00	$81.00	$117.45	$176.18	$14.68
$4.50	$54.00	$66.00	$89.10	$129.20	$193.79	$16.15
$5.00	$60.00	$72.00	$97.20	$140.94	$211.41	$17.62
$5.50	$66.00	$78.00	$105.30	$152.69	$229.03	$19.09

Column A	Column B	Column C	Column D	Column E	Column F	Column G
Bottle (USD)	Case (12 btl)	Clearance at $12 (USD)	Imp mrkup (FOB) x1.35	Wholesale x1.45	Retail/ cs (store) x1.5	Retail/ bottle
$6.00	$72.00	$84.00	$113.40	$164.43	$246.65	$20.55
$6.50	$78.00	$90.00	$121.50	$176.18	$264.26	$22.02
$7.00	$84.00	$96.00	$129.60	$187.92	$281.88	$23.49
$7.50	$90.00	$102.00	$137.70	$199.67	$299.50	$24.96
$8.00	$96.00	$108.00	$145.80	$211.41	$317.12	$26.43
$8.50	$102.00	$114.00	$153.90	$223.16	$334.73	$27.89
$9.00	$108.00	$120.00	$162.00	$234.90	$352.35	$29.36

I have tried to make the graph as simple as possible, by excluding all exchange rates and simply starting with USD. It is easy to take the Euro, Peso, Koruna or Lev and convert it into the US Dollar exchange rate of that time, if you are quoting in your local currency.

- **Column A:** the price per bottle in US Dollars.
- **Column B:** the price per 12 bottle (9L) case.
- **Column C:** adding $12 to the case price is an average, although arbitrary, figure for freight, duty and excise taxes, for purposes of this chart. This will vary considerably but some figure must be factored into pricing, based on where the wine is originating from, whether it lands at port of final destination or has to go overland, if it's a reefer, or whether it is Less Than Container Load (LCL). I have based the $12 on comfortably covering expenses for most FCL, including a thermal liner or bin liner for insulation and marine insurance. Since it becomes your importer's responsibility in most situations, he or she may not discuss this with you, but it is something you benefit from knowing as an element in pricing from winery to consumer.
- **Column D:** importer markup is generally in the 35% range, although this also can vary depending upon whether the importer anticipates a particular volume and has placed their margin lower to meet a target price point, or if they have an aggressive marketing campaign, high overhead with staff and other factors. It is entirely their decision as to what this markup becomes and there are many expenses included in the markup, so I can assure you the net profit margin becomes only a fraction of this.

- **Column E:** this is an example of a typical distributor markup percentage, in this case 45%, although these days it is not uncommon to see 50%. Again, not something set in stone and also not something anyone else has any control over, nonetheless important to know. It is noteworthy that the wholesaler (distributor) often has the largest overhead of the three tiers, including their own warehouse to store a large and varied inventory, office staff, sales team, local taxes, delivery personnel, trucking fuel and so on. But they are also likely to have the highest sales volume, based on a more extensive portfolio and larger individual sales than a retailer. Most sales staff will be on commission, but may also have a salary base and company benefits.

  Also of note, if your importer is also the distributor in their home state they have two markups (and margins) to work with, which should benefit them considerably, although overhead will also increase. This is an opportunity for your importer to utilize more marketing budget, take control of their distribution and have a cushion in the case of promotions and other incentives. You should keep in mind, though, that most importers will also be selling outside their state to other wholesalers and must keep prices consistent. While it appears they are most likely operating with an advantageous margin in-state, this will not be the case elsewhere. These days, it is easy for anyone to compare pricing online.

- **Column F:** the retail markup to the consumer, the price the end buyer pays for the wine. Based on factors such as size of retail operation—that is large, warehouse-sized chain to local, boutique shop—the markup could vary from 14% (Costco) to 60% for the high end, small shop with a wine bar where they offer daily wine tastings for free. However, the 50% I used in this table is to bring the table to a conclusion to show a retail price and that's really what you want to see: what price will my wine sell to the consumer, on average? Does it meet a goal? Does it, for example, retail for <$10 or is it a comparable price to my competitor's wine?

- **Column G:** this is simply the individual bottle price, taken from the case price of Column F.

Positioning

Understanding the mechanism to get from FOB to retail also allows you to see in which range you, or your importer, would ideally like to position the wine. If you are only a few points off your target price—that is $9.99, $12.99 or $19.99—then you can see how adjusting your selling price will advance this goal. Remember, this is a range. In various states, taxes, markups, cost of living and other factors might mean a difference of $1 or more per bottle in the retail price. Additionally, keep in mind that the retail price indicated in this table (and in any calculations using markup), will not be the price on the shelf. If you look at Column G, you will see prices at $8.81, $14.68 and $24.63, just to use examples. These will most likely become $8.99, $14.99 and $24.99, respectively. If you consider the prices $16.15, $19.09 and $22.02, the retailer could price them at $15.99, $18.99 and $21.99 respectively. However, this will depend on the retailer's margin and how they want to position the wines themselves and they could easily end up as $16.99, $19.99 and $22.99. Where you and your importer see your wine on the shelf or what will make a difference to a sale is all part of your positioning.

The same applies when selling wine to restaurants. If your importer wants to go after 'by the glass' wine sales in a restaurant, rather than bottle placements on the wine list, pricing is critical and may make the difference between the restaurant selling one bottle a month and selling three cases a week. There will be more discussion on this later in a bird's eye view of your importer's distribution efforts.

On the other hand, if initial response, low production levels and accolades indicate a need to price your wine as a premium product, then positioning becomes more about reaching an accord with your importer, who will in turn communicate the business and marketing plan to distributors. If demand is sufficiently high and supply sufficiently limited, this will be a joint effort not to permit deep discounts, nor allow retailers to under-cut other sales outlets, thereby retaining pricing integrity.

Brand Launch

Incentives to promote wine sales are an integral part of doing business in the U.S. It is not essential to most brands' success, but if it is in your budget and your wines' retail price point is sensitive, then prepare for this question from your importer in anticipating the brand's launch. You can be assured that most distributors will ask your importer the same thing, at least in states where it is legal. Marketing support is not a mandatory component to selling wine in the U.S. by any means, but it has become more and more customary as a way to differentiate brands in a crowded market. If you are able to afford it, have established this as part of your business plan, or built a cushion into your price, a financial marketing contribution is something to contemplate as part of a brand launch. This, however, raises other questions:

- Will the importer contribute to the launch incentive?

    In other words, will they also match it with funds of their own, or a temporary discount.

- Are you guaranteed that whatever amount you allocate to a brand launch will be utilized for this purpose?

    You may have agreed to augment the sample allowance for the first order, for example, or to discount off invoice for marketing support. Be sure to make it clear to the importer that this discount is specifically designated for this purpose. Most importers will be quite responsible about it, but it is also easy for anyone to take it for granted as part of the price.

- Is there accountability?

    No winery, importer, distributor or retailer can ever truly quantify their marketing or advertising efforts, but you should be able to learn how the funds or samples allocated to a marketing launch were utilized and be given some broad idea of the outcome. This will not only ensure the appropriate use of your incentives, but could also guide your future efforts to promote your brand.

    Down the line, the importer should be asking the same questions of the distributor.

- What is the distributor prepared to do to partner with the importer in introducing the brand?

    For the greatest likelihood of success, the distributor must also become invested in the outcome of the brand launch. The importer has already demonstrated a significant commitment by spending time and resources sourcing your wines, most likely traveling to your location and meeting with you, attending to logistical and compliance arrangements and shipping and warehousing, not to mention paying for a significant volume of wine. It is in the importer's best interests to invest further to ensure a return on investment.

The distributor, however, makes a much smaller investment in product that is readily available from the importer to ascertain whether this brand will sell in their marketplace. If it doesn't, they can easily move on to the next new line. In fairness, distributors may not always have the budget to dedicate funds to incentives at the time they take on a brand, however enthusiastic and committed they may be. But, as in all business relationships, the most committed parties have a vested interest in the outcome. If the distributor shares equally in a mutually agreed incentive program, the more likely they are to encourage and monitor their sales staff.

Distributors will sometimes commit personnel and marketing resources to a launch, either in place of or in addition to a monetary contribution, such as making your brand a priority for all sales staff for the first month. This gives an extra boost to the launch while the product is fresh to the market and the salespeople, and it also gives the distributor an early perspective on how well the wines are likely to perform.

The downside to relying on the sales staff is that the brand may not initially perform well, which may be more indicative of the effort put forth than it is a forecast of the brand's future performance. It is therefore incumbent on your importer to work on the brand's behalf either behind the scenes or in concert with the distributor. This is an area in which you will have little control, but it is a part of the U.S. wine world culture that is helpful for you to understand as part of the dialogue with your importer.

Although you may be disinclined or unable to provide incentives or a marketing budget to your importer at this early stage, it is also useful to know how promotions in general are viewed by your importer. It is important, for instance, that initial incentives are short-term and designed to generate immediate results. There is nothing less likely to motivate distributors and their sales teams over the life of the brand as a program that is taken for granted as a static component of the price. My suggestion to importers operating with a modest budget, and I have done this myself, is to offer incentives on the first order, perhaps of free goods (where legal) or a modest contest. Therefore, the term of the launch incentives could be limited to either:

- The first order
- The first month
- The current quarter
- When a certain dollar sales volume is reached
- When a designated number of accounts are established

Incentives can be modest or lavish, depending on the budget. It can be one case of free goods on a pallet (or equivalent discount) or a contest for a trip to the brand's country of origin. Whatever the incentive, it must be logical, meaningful and easily quantifiable. The launch of a product cannot bankrupt the importer. If a brand's volume potential is sufficiently large, and there is across-the-board involvement in funding a trip with air fare and accommodations at the winery, for example, this is an exciting way to get started. But if the brand's volume or price point is quite moderate, then it makes no sense to offer a trip that exceeds any reasonable profits to be made from the program.

There is also nothing worse than a program that either cannot be understood, and will therefore be ignored, or where there is no discernible way to monitor the results of the incentives. A clear and simple proposal and accountability are both key.

Additionally, the incentive program must be tailored to the circumstances: state, region, distributor's resources, desirability of your brand, ease of selling or contemporary expectations. For example, if the program is to offer $5 for every case sold, this may be a thoroughly appropriate incentive for an inexpensive wine that is likely to be case-stacked in stores and generate volume. On the other hand, your importer may offer $5 a case for a wine that is high priced, unknown and difficult to sell, when, in this particular wholesale house, they are accustomed to incentives of $20 a case. There should be no pressure to match this type of programming. Incentives for the launch of your brand should be customized to the situation with an expectation of reasonable results. If your importer sees that an incentive program with a particular wholesaler doesn't make financial sense because of the outlay it requires, then they must find another way to promote and support your brand.

It is quite possible to establish and grow your brand on its attributes alone, along with your importer's judicious management and fostering of relationships within the ranks of the distributor's salespeople. Within that framework (if legal in that state), they can also take the opportunity to pass along samples they receive from you, their supplier, as an incentive.

* * *

Final Thoughts

It should now become clear why it is so important to find an importer who will be far more than just someone in the U.S. who has agreed to purchase and sell your wines. This partnership relies on respect, like-minded thinking and an ability for each party to take on faith that the other has their best interests at heart. In some cases, it means deferring to your importer's greater experience and familiarity with the U.S. and in other instances your importer should recognize when your decisions must prevail. An importer must be free to set pricing and orchestrate the launch at their end, but often a compromise can be reached that satisfies both parties in the case of marketing, incentives and positioning the brand.

Part III

11

A Long Distance Relationship

You said goodbye to your wine, it is now in the hands of your customer and it's time to turn your attention to other matters, right? Wrong! Unlike machine parts or peaches, this carefully shepherded, hard-won sale is just the beginning of what you hope will be a beautiful relationship.

There are many ways in which you can be instrumental in seeing that this relationship thrives; some involve fully engaging and others require stepping back. But before undertaking any role in this relationship, it would be beneficial to understand the foundation your importer is laying to establish and facilitate sales.

Vetting the Distributor

If you recall, your importer can only sell wines to the retail trade, should he or she choose to do so legally, within their own home state. Otherwise, they must sell to distributors (wholesalers) in the remaining 49 states, or whatever prearranged area the two of you have worked out. Your importer may be a large, well-oiled machine with many moving parts and a distribution network established over many years. But very often your importer will be someone small to medium, perhaps with a limited, solid portfolio willing to take a chance on a new brand. The best importer of any size, without an entrenched distribution network willing to take on a series of new brands, will thoroughly investigate a potential buyer for your wines and a potential partner for the brand. Only someone desperate for business will take a haphazard approach. This may result in a sale, but may also mean more time will be spent in chasing additional sales and possibly payment. It is never worth cutting corners in this business. So what will your importer want in a distributor:

- A company with the same general business philosophy as theirs
- A financially sound business
- Terms that are reasonable—30-60 days usually, and they stick to it
- A company that covers the desired geographical area—that is it could be only one small territory of one state, or in the case of New York, for example, it's often preferable if they cover New Jersey as well
- Management that communicates well and is accessible
- A company that has a plan to invest in your brand and is willing to take a position across the board, instead of cherry-picking
- A company that has the skill and expertise to represent the wines appropriately, with familiarity with the region or a demonstrated understanding of the wines
- Focused management and sales people
- A portfolio that may include your country or region, but is not saturated and therefore creating unwarranted competition within the portfolio
- A company not so large that the brand gets lost amid the demands and quotas forced upon them by bigger companies

The U.S. is a nation of fifty different wine fiefdoms and operates very differently from the blurred borders of the European Union or the relaxed regulations of much of the rest of the world. However, through thorough investigation, connections and making use of contacts it is possible to find the right fit not only once, but throughout the country.

Brokers

I bring this to your attention because brokers can often be another selling arm for the importer, both by finding a fully vetted distributor on their behalf and by following up on sales, placements and distributor sales team's activity within the state. But you should also understand that brokers charge on average a 10% commission for their services (to the importer) to be paid after the invoice funds are remitted to the importer from the distributor. Occasionally, brokers charge a higher percentage or a retainer, but it is not customary and there should be some extraordinary circumstances to warrant the additional cost. A broker commission adds yet another layer to the importer's pricing, making it essentially a *four* tier system, instead of the already burdensome three, or cuts 10% from your importer's margin. But this arrangement can also add sales that otherwise might not have been available, so it is a matter of weighing the advantages.

A broker can be beneficial because a smaller importer, especially one without an established distribution network, can't be everywhere and do everything. In addition to actually approaching a distributor on the importer's behalf, usually someone they know well, they can add momentum to the brand's distribution, often working with the salespeople, holding independent tastings and generally shepherding the brand within the territory.

In Control states (that is those where wine sales are "controlled" by the government and not free enterprise) a broker can be invaluable and actually a necessity. They know the players, that is, the government buyers, understand what they may be looking for and what they are not looking for, when a particular country's wines are scheduled to come up on the State's tasting calendar, how to monitor sales in specialty stores and manage reorders and generally perform functions that an importer is unable to accomplish.

The right broker can often save the importer money, despite their commission, by limiting the quantity of samples going out to prospective customers, lessening the number of visits needed to the market, and working with the distributor's sales people to keep your brand at the forefront of their attention.

The right broker will also be honest with an importer about the assessment of your wines by the various distributors or retailers, have an ear to the ground for which wines are likely to be in demand, and be poised to recommend a switch if they see a negative trend in the current wholesale house.

Of course, this is only an option for an importer, not a prerequisite for doing business. In many states and with many established importers, it is not necessary. In fact, importers with considerable sales turnover will have their own national sales team or salaried, regional managers. This is the preferable arrangement, guaranteeing a singular focus on the importer's brands, but takes an importer budget and distribution scope that can support this type of overhead.

Sample Usage—Publications

Samples are such a necessary part of the process from the very beginning and continue throughout the life of the wines. Samples begin a dialogue with a potential buyer—in the first instance between you and your importer. As previously mentioned, they are also utilized by your importer to submit to publications. Samples were once a tool for importers to pre-select wines, before any commitment was made, but in more recent times the noted and most influential wine publications have refused to review wines that were not already in U.S. distribution. By refusing to accept bottles unless they already have U.S. compliant labels, wine publications are ensuring that importers have not agreed to represent brands solely on the basis of high U.S. ratings. This presumes that the importer has already committed to the wines by going through the COLA (Certificate of Label Approval) process and the winery has committed to the importer by having labels printed for the U.S. market. Not a very scientific process, but better than it used to be when anyone could submit any wines, irrespective of whether they were ever intended for the U.S. market.

Depending upon the wines, their origin, pricing, quality, expectations and other factors that should be left up to your importer, the major wine publications would be:

- Wine Spectator
- Wine Enthusiast
- Wine & Spirits
- Wine Advocate

For these publications, guidelines change all the time. As of 2014, due to the volume of wines submitted to their offices, Wine Spectator requires an email submission of wine information *before* submitting samples to their Napa office. According to Tom Matthews, Executive Editor, "As the number of wines seeking reviews increased - dramatically over the past few years, I might add—we were winding up having to deal with bottles that could not be reviewed, both because they did not meet our criteria and because we simply didn't have the logistical capacity.

We do not intend to review fewer wines; in fact, we increased the number of official reviews from 17,300 in 2012 to 20,500 in 2014. But that is still only a fraction of the wines released in the US each year, and also a fraction of the number of wines that request to be reviewed by Wine Spectator. Our new policy is intended to give us more thoughtful control over the wines we review, to ensure that we balance coverage of the world's important regions and give guidance to our readers about the wines that are important to them.

For wines produced outside the US, our baseline policy is to review wines only if they have official US importers, and if those importers formally request reviews. We can't accept samples directly from international producers, nor do we want to spend the energy to review wines that are not available to our US readers, the bulk of our circulation.

We hope our new policies will help avoid inefficiencies for everyone involved in the supply chain and enable us to improve our ability to review the wines are readers are most interested in".

Beyond the above mentioned periodicals, there are other influential national and local magazines and newspapers that might be receptive and would deliver good exposure. These include the New York Times, The San Francisco Chronicle, The Dallas Morning News, The Wall Street Journal and Food and Wine Magazine. There are others of course, but these are prominent publications that could provide opportunities. This is all for your information only. It will be the responsibility of your importer to pursue these prospects. These days, a number of wine bloggers can often be as, or more, influential than some publications and the importer should be aware of the traffic and impact individuals may have. Samples can provide an enormous boost to sales, but should always be used prudently with a view to the potential return.

In general, print media and ratings are in varying degrees of decline. However, this does not mean they cannot be influential, especially since traditional print media has increased their online presence. Submitting to publications is free publicity, and good ratings can make the difference on a retail wine shelf or in approaching a distributor.

For most publications, expect to wait at least six months for a review to appear. Sometimes it is because of the sheer volume of submissions. In other instances magazines require submissions to coincide with an issue that focuses on a particular country's wine. This can be very frustrating to both you and the importer, but ratings are only one tool in the toolbox. There are many activities the importer will be engaged in simultaneously in an effort to establish the brand.

In the event of a high rating, you will be aware of the status of your wine without inquiring, even some months in advance. Wine Spectator will not disclose the rating in advance, but will tip their hand to some degree by contacting your importer to request a label to include with the review (free of charge). Wine Enthusiast and Wine & Spirits will send an email to the importer with the rating included, asking whether they wish to submit a label (for an advertising fee) as an accompaniment to the wine's review.

Some people are of the opinion that a good rating in some of these publications, such as Wine Enthusiast, is dependent upon this advertising supplement, but I know from personal experience that this is not the case. First of all, the publication notifies the importer of the rating prior to soliciting a label insertion fee. The fee is entirely optional, and the rating does not change when advertising is declined. Others suggest that Wine Spectator gives favor to the big advertisers in their publication, but I have had some very high ratings in this magazine and never advertised. I think the personal palate bias that is inescapable in any taster's review of a wine has more to do with the rating variable than anything else. Certainly a wine is either well-made or deficient, true to its varietal, its heritage and expectations of the vintage or not, but beyond that there has to be, even in some indefinable, unconscious way, a tendency to rate higher or lower because the wine fits, or does not fit, a personal preference. We are all human. It is an imperfect, subjective system but it serves a purpose. Some consumers have learned to trust one palate over another as more closely aligned with their own, which still means there is some value in a rating.

Conversely, when the rating is poor in one publication, it will not be included in the wine's publicity, but a certain word or phrase may be sufficiently positive that not all is thrown out. And if the wines have been submitted to several publications and some are given higher worth, then this is the review or rating that becomes part of your importer's marketing efforts.

Sample Usage—Pre-Selling

Pre-selling is an optional but potentially important early task for your importer. If you elect to airfreight wine prior to shipping the container, it allows the importer to jump-start the order process by sending samples to fully vetted distributors allowing them an opportunity to develop sales prior to the shipment's arrival. Air freight is a fairly expensive proposition, however, and may not be feasible or in your budget. But this process is usually only necessary once. In later containers, new release wines can be put in the container along with the order and save you the expense of an air shipment.

If you do send samples ahead of the purchased wines, or if the importer has the opportunity to bring some back with them from a visit, you can feel confident that they will be put to good use because it can make such a difference to the importer's business model. The process of seeking, attracting and selling all takes far longer than you can imagine and certainly far longer than most importers want to spend with the clock ticking on storage charges and the rest of their overhead while they wait to sell wines and receive payment. Being able to identify interested wholesalers or contacting those they may have worked with before and sending requested samples means that your importer can slightly shorten this sequence of events. Here is an example of a scenario at the outset of the distribution process in the U.S. It will be repeated many times across the country as importers look for opportunities throughout the fifty states with the right wholesaler. It goes like this:

- Research, narrow down and vet a distributor
- Make contact via phone (preferable) or email if necessary
- Continue to follow up until there is a response (or move on when there is none)
- Send pricing and any other information they request
- Wait for a response
- Follow up when sufficient time has elapsed
- Send samples, only at their request, when it has been determined that there is serious interest
- Wait for the wines to be tasted—this could be either at a Friday morning sales meeting with the team, at a management meeting, after other samples in the queue have been tasted, or when there is time
- Once a decision is made, wait for a purchase order
- Allow time for a pickup of the order

This process can take many months and tax the most patient person, but it is par for the course in the U.S. and everyone in the wine industry becomes accustomed to operating within these parameters. The key is to have many such contacts and processes going on all the time so that while you and the importer are waiting for one distributor to make a decision, there are simultaneous strategies in play in other states and a progression of sales can be taking place. Intense competition has made it quite challenging to do business, but the intrepid, dogged importer can achieve success with the right brands and approach.

Sample Usage—Wholesaler/Distributor

Wines will not get sold without sampling; this is a simple truth. Except perhaps in the case of specifically allocated, tiny production, highly rated, expensive wines, which may be pre-sold to special accounts on the basis of their rarefied desirability. In the case of just about everything else, the customer tastes the wines and decides accordingly. It may be hard to comprehend, but just as your sale to your importer doesn't stop at the port, neither does their expenditure on samples to the distributor. It is another industry norm that samples used by the distributor and its salespeople are at least partly the responsibility of the importer. The importer must pay attention to sample usage, since indiscriminate use, with no accountability, creates an untenable situation.

Most distributors will find the convention of sharing equally in the cost of samples to be acceptable and customary. Samples are handled through a statement called a "bill-back," which should be sent monthly or quarterly to the importer from the distributor. The distributor must send this report on a regular basis to allow the importer to incorporate samples costs into their budget or put the brakes on over-sampling if insufficient sales are generated from the sample usage.

If salespeople are inhibited by sample limits, they will be less likely to promote your wines. If they can't sample they can't sell. They may take the wines out for a certain period of time and then stop. After all, the wholesale house will either discourage the use of samples, or require the salesperson to be responsible for their own sample costs if the supplier is applying sample quotas.

The other customary practice with samples—so much so as to be an industry norm—is for the distributor to charge 100% bill-back on the following:

- Spoiled product (generally corked wine)
- When the supplier (either the importer or you, the brand owner) works the market
- Trade shows

An unwritten code seems to have developed around the use of trade show and supplier visit samples, presumably because they are not dispensed at the distributor's discretion and out of the distributor's control.

I always suggest that an importer make comparisons across the country of sample usage vs. sales. It is not scientific, but often helpful in zeroing in on aberrations, which can be brought to the attention of the distributor. It also helps the importer evaluate a particular distributor's effectiveness.

Incentives

This is an area in which your importer may not involve you, but helpful for you to know about in having an overall understanding of the market. To me, *brand launch* incentives and *ongoing* incentive programs are quite different. The goal of the initial stages is to start buzz for an unknown brand, unknown at least to the newly appointed distributor. The timing is certainly designed to set an optimistic tone for the success of the product. Later, it's about stimulating sales. Sales may have languished, the brand is getting lost amid new offerings or big brand quotas, or you are ready for a vintage change and your importer needs to make room.

There are states in which incentives, also known as programming, are illegal and in the ones where it is legal, some inducements work better than others. An importer should be guided primarily by their contact at the distributor—whether it is the hands-on owner, sales manager or top salesperson—someone with whom they have established a close connection and they can rely on for his or her input. This individual really does know what works and what doesn't and how easily it can be managed, given their sales team or their territory.

The programming put in place after the launch should be at least for a calendar quarter (three months), in my opinion. It can even run all year for a high value contest, but a quarter should keep interest high and attention focused while also allowing a sufficient period to realize a significant sales bump. For more immediate impact, with high expectations and perhaps tied in with wine dinners and tastings, a month or even a week can be appropriate. This is most often implemented when you, or your winemaker if this is a different entity, is in town.

Incentives can additionally be divided into two categories:

- Those to the salesperson
- Those to the on-premise (restaurant) and off-premise (retailer)

In other words, the programming of choice may benefit the salesperson directly in the form of cash, prizes or trips, or indirectly in terms of free goods to the retailer or a by-the-glass program (wines poured by the glass, rather than sold by the bottle) pricing for the restaurant. Both benefit the salesperson, but operate quite differently.

The salesperson programming can also be further sub-divided into two categories:

- On-premise sales
- Off-premise sales

This is another one of those important distinctions because if a program is instituted for volume, for example, the on-premise salesperson cannot compete with the level of sales. The off-premise salesperson (if the distributor sets their staffing or territories up this way) may be able to sell fifteen cases of a product to one retail account whereas the on-premise salesperson will need fifteen accounts (or twenty if split cases are allowed) to accomplish the same thing. The ongoing sales benefit and exposure of the glass pour at a restaurant may far outweigh the one-time sale to the retail account, but it cannot be quantified in the initial programming period.

Suggestions for programming incentives include the following.

Launch or Pre-Sell

- 3% sample allowance deducted from invoice or included in free goods across brands
- Large format (1.5L or 3L) bottles as percentage of order or "prizes" for performance
- $5 for each new wine placement on-premise
- $5 for each case in a minimum 3 case stack off-premise
- $20 for by-the-glass placements (with minimum time frame or case purchase)

The importer will be guided by the distributor and the circumstances, but must be aware that they may be setting a precedent for future orders that they may not wish, or be able, to fulfill. They must not fall into the trap of being expected to include standard free goods or sample allowance deduction on each shipment or invoice. This will become absorbed into the price and taken for granted, instead of being used as liberal tasting samples, as it should be.

Ongoing Off-Premise

- "One case on ten" that is, one case free for every ten cases sold—one quarter time period
- "One case on 13" that is, one case free for every thirteen cases purchased. The logic of this is that fourteen cases is a "layer" on a pallet. As a pallet in the U.S. is fifty-six cases, this is divided into four layers of fourteen cases each. Very often a distributor may say, "I'll take a layer of xxx wine"—as part of an order.
- $15 per each (min.) 3 case stack—one quarter
- $200 gift certificate for highest volume sales over the designated sales period—one quarter
- Contest for specified elements of a trip to the country or region of origin for the brand in question. This may be airfare, with the winner visiting or, if feasible, staying at your winery or on the estate and then on their own for the rest of the trip. It may be an organized, accompanied, all expenses paid trip. Recommended contest period for something of this nature would naturally be within budget parameters, but twelve months would be a reasonable timeframe. Since this is an extended program, the importer must make sure the sales or brand manager is keeping everyone abreast of progress and it stays at the forefront of their minds.

Ongoing On-Premise

- $20 for glass pour placement—3 case minimum
- $10 for wine list placement
- Same as above trip contest, but with requirements that are tailored to on-premise parameters, such as number of wine or glass pour placements or hotel or chain placements.

There are some inherent pitfalls in understanding what the glass pour or by-the-glass program entails for restaurant placements, which is why a minimum order or time period is spelled out.

A program will have far more impact when the wholesaler matches your importer's incentive, so that instead of $5 a case, it becomes $10. Instead of a $200 gift certificate, it can become $400. Not only is the distributor more invested, but the sales person is obviously more motivated to sell your wine.

If you, as a brand owner, are in a position to invest something in programming as well, this can be a powerful tool to help overcome the challenges of distributors with languishing inventories, too much competition and/or overworked or apathetic salespeople. If not, this section has at least allowed you to appreciate the type of business that is customarily conducted at this level.

Below is just one example of an incentive I used for a brand that happened to have a number of large format bottles of various varietals and vintages, expressly for the purpose of prizes and gifts:

INCENTIVE EXAMPLES FOR MARKETING VISIT BY WINERY FOR A SPECIFIED PERIOD

(Specify dollar amount or reward) or one Magnum for each of the following:

- *Two Reps that sell the most dollars of all Brand X*
- *Two Reps that sell the most cases of all Brand X*
- *One Rep that sells the most cases of Brand X's wine #1*
- *The First Rep to produce an email offer for off-premise account- min two products (see below for account bonus)*
- *The First Rep to produce a feature Brand X dinner (see below for account bonus)*

One Brand X Magnum to the ACCOUNT (sales rep to validate)

- *First to produce a Brand X Dinner*
- *First Brand X products (at least two) in a newsletter*
- *The first on-premise account to order 5 cases of Brand X's wine #1 for BTG (copy of wine list required and invoices)*

You will note that the incentive program was two-fold; the first was to motivate the sales reps and the second, to encourage accounts to participate, doubling the potential for success. This does not necessarily mean that this type of programming works best in all circumstances. It was only one type that I used over many years and the availability of desirable magnums made it possible. These were also generally highly rated wines and the brand had a broad range of wines from which to choose.

Communication

The U.S. may be the most important market for you, or it may not. Either way, it will at least be at the forefront of your focus in the beginning because you have worked so hard to secure it (and I know you have) or it becomes of utmost importance to keep it. To that end, you may be motivated to communicate frequently with your new importer. This can arise from a sense that you want to encourage them, ensure that your wines stay at the forefront of *their* focus, or because you are concerned that they won't be doing enough unless you are there to prod them. None of this is likely to be true. As I've said before, your importer has invested a considerable amount of time, effort and money to develop this relationship and their focus will be entirely on making it work. Since it is difficult to make a living from just one brand, unless yours is a multi-level, high volume, value series of wines, the importer will also have many other tasks they must perform. Concurrently, they may be launching your brand, traveling to another state for a trade show, responding to purchase orders, arranging for a container and overseeing brand managers or brokers.

Your goal should be to communicate sufficiently to demonstrate interest and commitment, but not so often that your importer is cringing every time they hear your voice. Yes, you and your brand are very important to them, but unless each conversation with you yields valuable information they can use to further sales, it is time they could spend actually selling wine. You don't want to communicate with pressure or inappropriate requests. Nor do want to leave your importer to their own devices and only communicate when you need something. But you do want to communicate.

This can be a fairly fluid component, depending upon the importer's needs and the dynamics of their company. At one end of the spectrum is someone who expects you to schedule quarterly trips to the U.S., call and email constantly with updates, send samples of new product and vintages upon release and be prepared to offer regular discounts and incentives. At the other end you have an importer who basically wants you to leave them alone to do their job and make one visit a year for a productive trip to key markets.

The first example is deliberately excessive to illustrate an extreme, but not so far off that it doesn't represent a certain type of importer. This is why it is so important to get to know one another before the first sale, to see if this is the type of relationship you feel is worth supporting. The level of support you provide—in time and money—should be commensurate with what you get back from your importer in terms of orders. But initially, it is important to make known your desire to be a team player and allow the relationship to develop in an appropriate way. If you find that the orders only come when you work the market, and only to the extent of the sales you made while you were there, then this is not a partnership. Essentially, you are the only one working and the subsequent sales may not be worth the cost of the travel and incentive deals.

At that other end of the spectrum, where the importer basically wants you to leave them alone, it is still in your best interests to be a contributing member of this collaboration. It is vital to provide your importer with appropriate sales tools to enable them to maximize their efforts. Leaving them entirely on their own can also result in forgetting about your brand or finding another primary brand focus in their portfolio.

- If you have new press, be sure to send it.
- Offer to come and work the market at a suitable time
- Let them know when a product level is low, or when the next harvest or bottling will take place
- Forward new trade tools, for example notable winery recognition, tasting notes for new vintages, harvest conditions or helpful background details

All of this can be accomplished via email, of course, with the occasional phone call when a discussion will accomplish more. Leaving your importer entirely alone perpetuates a misconception that you are only marginally interested in them and their market, and eventually they may only become marginally interested in you and your wines.

* * *

Final Thoughts

As you can see from this chapter, the foundation you establish from the beginning in terms of support, communication and guidance—both from and to your importer—can set the stage for the future. An investment in your U.S. distribution should be considered as part of the big picture and not on the basis of what it costs you at the outset. Samples, for example, are not a large investment, but can make a huge difference to your importer's business. I have experienced the gamut of material support and volume of samples and worked with whatever I'm given or the producer could afford. I am aware that small vineyards are often struggling to reach the next level of production and sales. But if you do have sales resources at your disposal, it may help you to appreciate the reasoning behind your importer's requests. It is short-sighted to want to rein in the spending in the beginning when this is just the start of a long term commitment.

Keeping the Momentum Going

I think we've established that making a sale to a U.S. importer is not the end of the transaction. On the other hand, you cannot expect your importer to focus 100% of their attention on your brand by focusing all their attention on your needs. Unless the arrangement you have is a joint partnership or your wines are the only ones in the portfolio, all other relationships are symbiotic in the sense that you are assisting each other for the mutual benefit of ongoing sales. And as such, both must balance the needs of the other.

Supporting Short Term Goals
This next part reflects on what your importer might require at the outset of the relationship and the launch of your brand. Each stage may trigger another opportunity to examine the same concepts from a different perspective. We've already covered some of the communication and inventory topics that will arise and how anticipating needs will smooth the path for both of you. Much of the preceding will be relevant irrespective of personalities, business practices and style. But supporting your individual importer's initial, short-term approach to launching your brand will

depend very much on subjective circumstances and these are some of the questions that may arise:

- Have they requested marketing support?
- Are you in a position to supply it?
- Does it make sense to you—both financially and for the brand?
- What is the intended outcome?
- How much impact is projected short-term and long-term?
- What is the likely outcome without it? (There may be none.)
- Has the importer articulated and quantified the support and intended outcome to your satisfaction?

Again, there is no right or wrong approach to marketing support, only right or wrong for you. The point is to look at the situation and prepare your response. The early stages are critical to the brand, first impressions are important, and your importer will have a hundred different tasks to perform at once. Your primary concern will be what they intend to do with your wine when it arrives and how you can aid the launch.

They may ask you for assistance, tangible or intangible, or they may ask you to wait to hear from them, but ultimately (except for a monetary request from you), it will be their decision as to the right preliminary approach and initially you should respect that they have a plan and will execute it.

Market Visit Timing

This is another subjective matter, both for you and for the importer and, in this instance, one into which you can reasonably have considerable input. It is a very expensive proposition to make a trip from wherever you are traveling to the States, no matter how near or far away your home. In addition to airfare, you will have accommodations, your own meals, others' meals, internal travel arrangements, wine and so on. Market visits are something that are often hard to quantify in terms of financial success and yet are almost *essential* to the success of the brand and its identity in the U.S., when taking into consideration the impact you are trying to make on all tiers of the distribution system, from importer, to distributor, to retailer, to consumer. Every one of them is conditioned to invest in a brand with which they can clearly and enthusiastically identify. These are some of the things you should consider prior to a market visit, or even prior to broaching the subject:

- Is the importer counting on you to come over from the outset to be the "face of the brand"?
- Are they determined to make significant inroads before any visit at all?
- Do they want to ensure that you have product placement prior to visiting those markets?
- Are they relying on your help to make the initial placements?
- Do they want you to make presentations to distributor's management or sales teams?
- Is this a short or long trip proposal?
- How many trips do they envision for you per year (or other criteria)?
- What is your schedule?
- What is your budget?
- What is your personality type? (More on that later.)
- What is your inclination regarding market visits?
- How long can you be away from family/vineyard/commitments?

Other factors to bring to the decision process might include:

- **Is this a new importer who is amassing their first portfolio?**

    If they have no distribution area and very few brands, under most circumstances my suggestion is to wait until they have an aggregate of both, making a trip to the U.S. much more meaningful in terms of number of markets to visit and a full schedule. Someone inexperienced may think your presence will be an advantage in approaching potential distributors, but this will not usually be the case. Distributors will make those decisions on the basis of need, available space, potential for placements and all the other issues that are inherent to the brand: price, packaging, quality and style of wine.

- **Is this an established importer who already has many brands in distribution?**

    The case could be made either way for a market visit now or to wait, but always with the same proviso: that the trip has to carry its own weight in terms of outcome. You are not there to have a holiday (unless you want to) or as a "meet and greet"; you are there to propel your brand into a sales pipeline.

- **Do they have well developed plans for launch?**

    If your presence could make a big difference to a synchronized introduction with planned dinners, tastings or trade shows, meeting of distribution principals where brand is placed, or other well-organized efforts where people are counting on your appearance as part of the marketing. Your participation should still be part of the conversations you have with your importer, to ensure your agreement and to coordinate with your schedule.

- **Have they done a good job of making substantial pre-sell placements?**

    In this case, sales have been made, there may be timing considerations for various markets, such as pre-holiday sales or a spring push and this may be the only trip you make all year.

- **Is their style to set it all in motion from their office?**

    This is often an importer's prerogative, especially a smaller company where the initial sales have been made via phone, email and samples and the distributor has asked them to wait until the wines are in the sales team's hands or some placements have been made.

- **Has the importer planned on visiting every market at the outset?**

    This could correspond to the importer's own plans for their travel and they intend to incorporate your brand's launch into their own schedule. Or if yours is a large volume brand that has made some significant inroads that requires the importer's presence at a sales team launch in each place, this may or may not include you.

- **Are there brokers, employees or brand ambassadors (the latter are usually 100% commission based marketers) in place to support the brand?**

    If this is the case, they should be the brand's first line into market and provide the necessary backing to ensure a successful introduction and follow through.

- **Does your importer already have concomitant obligations to attend to when launching your brand?**

    In other words, without knowing exactly when the last arrangements would be finalized and your brand arrives, they have carried on with the rest of their portfolio and have already made arrangements to attend events, make market visits for existing brands and attend to commitments to their existing suppliers and customers. In this case, it is best to wait, even if you are someone who is anxious to make a trip, because this will not be the best use of your time or your importer's. The established importer's workload involving other brands can be both an advantage and disadvantage for you. You should still have a discussion about ways in which you can make your brand a priority, or at least not lose momentum.

- **The new importer may not have yet developed the necessary relationship to set up a market visit at the launch or, alternatively, may really need your help sooner rather than later.**

    This is really self-explanatory and you should defer to their wishes. To do otherwise can only result in unrealized goals and unmet expectations.

- **If well-established (without prior commitments).**

    They should able to set up a visit for you by simply calling their close contacts at each wholesaler to establish a full schedule of events for you.

- **They may want their distributors to demonstrate a commitment to the program first.**

    By ordering and placing sufficient wines to demonstrate a solid relationship and worth putting time, effort and money into their market you show commitment. This way you avoid the initial "heavy lifting" of utilizing your time for those personal encounters that may end up being a wasted opportunity.

- **Your importer could initially discourage you from jumping on a plane to make that U.S. whirlwind market tour.**

    But you should also not allow them to dissuade you forever. Occasionally, you will find an importer who is unwilling to have the supplier "looking over their shoulder" or who could not be bothered to schedule an elaborate itinerary for their supplier. This is not the type of importer you want. It is always your decision as to whether you can afford to travel to the market or whether you want to (although at some point I highly encourage it), but an importer that never wants you to visit is a red flag.

- **Your importer could have brokers or brand managers in various markets.**

    This is a wonderful enhancement to the importer's sales efforts, if their budget allows, and an enormously effective tool to cut down on constant financial support and physical presence from either importer or winery, but in the eyes of the customer this will never take the place of a brand principal making a personal visit.

- **Your importer may have already asked for financial support for launch marketing.**

    This could cause you to decide between marketing dollars and your presence in the market. Budget is a consideration for most people and all importers recognize this. On the other hand, if you have committed funds for an initial launch, it becomes less critical for you to make the trip until a more convenient time.

- **Your importer may intend to make the initial trips to one, two or more states to ensure that they meet with key principals and participate directly in brand launch.**

    This is not necessarily a right or wrong approach, but it is one that means your immediate presence has not been factored into their plans.

Planning The Trip

Whether you are the producer who is chomping at the bit to come to the U.S. at regular intervals to be the face of the brand or the reluctant winemaker who is coaxed into making the trip at one crucial juncture for sales, there comes a time when a trip must be made, either to support the importer, to better understand how the market works, determine the course for your future in the U.S. or establish a clear identity for the brand. Making a trip is almost imperative for smaller brands, estate wines and those with which consumers most often want to make a connection. Otherwise, to the consumer at large your wines remain a sort of amorphous set that loses its ability to generate a loyal customer base.

I recall an Australian brand in the early days of my importing (not one of mine) that became so successful that people were going to Australia searching for the vineyard to visit. Unfortunately for them, no such vineyard existed. The brand was a negociant label sourced entirely for the U.S. market. In time, this happened with such frequency that the brand owners bought a vineyard and created a base for the brand and a destination for visitors. This was admittedly in the early days of intense Australian popularity, but it serves to illustrate the lengths to which people will go to make connections and seek out an experience associated with a wine or a brand.

On rare occasions, the supplier, who is often also the winemaker, will be absolutely convinced that their brand will somehow flounder and fail without their hands-on efforts, and that it is imperative to the success of the whole U.S. venture that they come over and shepherd its passage through the three-tier system, requiring extended, multi-city visits every quarter to accomplish this. I think this is an expensive exercise that often serves to satisfy the particular individual who wants a frequent holiday in the U.S. and to be fêted everywhere he or she goes. This is not a cost-effective way to market, unless the brand is now in millions of cases, and usually greatly interferes with the importer's own plans and scheduling. Although I have encountered two such individuals, both of whom lost their businesses, this is an extreme and only included to illustrate a point.

I always welcomed the supplier or representative because it helped me represent the brand, was often a way to visit markets that I may not have been able to accommodate at that time and usually resulted in increased sales. However, as a small importer with a range of family-owned vineyards and small brands, I usually discouraged a supplier from making the visit when the wine had just arrived or had just been launched. The wines' arrival meant a number of activities to attend to at once - registering the brand, perhaps obtaining new state licenses, getting samples out, researching more distributors, making sales and capitalizing on what may have been vital seasonal timing. Once the supplier enters that particular mix, the importer also becomes a travel agent and event planner and sometimes their own carefully laid plans must go on hold. There also may not be much a winery representative can do, given the limited number of markets that have the wine and depending on whether these markets are ready for their own launch at that particular time.

As for the reluctant supplier, I once represented a brand for over ten years and not once did the winery owner, who was also the winemaker, make a trip to the U.S. It was a good, solid brand from an organic vineyard, but it would undoubtedly have benefited from his appearance. If nothing else, he would have witnessed the changing U.S. palate and updated his wines accordingly. The wines were excellent quality, but somewhat old-fashioned and without updating to suit changing palates, sales eventually suffered.

So, while I encourage most winemakers/owners to visit because you are one degree less of separation—the actual people who have their hands in the soil and their feet in the juice, so to speak—the timing has to be right. If scheduled properly, with notice and generally not in the middle of summer, your presence will usually be welcomed by your importer, and distributors will make space for you and put considerable effort into seeing that your time is well spent in their market.

Trip Planning Logistics

As for the actual logistics, always plan in concert with your importer. Notice is vital, for both the importer who will be arranging your schedule and for the distributors, retailers and restaurants that will be hosting events for you. In many cases, it may be the importer who will need your presence and assistance at certain times for trade events and releases. In these instances, allowances must be made for your schedule and unavoidable conflicts like harvest, so communicating in advance when you are not available will be important to your importer.

You may have definite ideas about which states and cities you wish to visit, but these may not necessarily be the ones where the importer has distribution. Most suppliers will say they want to be in New York, Chicago and Los Angeles, for example, and this is, of course, understandable. Similarly, markets such as Houston, Miami and San Francisco may be on your list. But it will all depend on where your importer has achieved distribution and is able to ensure that your time is put to the best use. Texas, New York, New Jersey, Florida, California and Illinois are well known as the hottest markets for wine, with the highest wine consumption. Naturally, this means that everyone entering this country's wine market is targeting these states for their wines. The competition is fierce and not all will prevail. In addition, consider that the East Coast is, to use a generalization, more disposed towards European wines because of their region's immigration history and proximity to Europe. And the West Coast is inclined towards New World wines, again because of proximity and also because those styles are usually more aligned with the wines that California, in particular, produces. In the Midwest, the center of the country that is called the "breadbasket" of the nation, there is a large Central and Eastern Europe population whose tastes often harken back to the countries of their origin. Of course, there is significant crossover and people on both coasts who appreciate many different styles of wines, but when considering where your importer may have established sales or would like you to go to promote your wines, there are often reasons beyond the "hot" wine consumption states, so keep an open mind.

Despite whatever familiarity you may have with the U.S., you will not necessarily know where to stay, what connections to make, how long you need in each place and many other details. The Marriott downtown may not necessarily be the best choice. It could be the little inn closest to the rep you'll be working with, or the hotel near the wholesaler's headquarters on the other side of town.

Establish at the outset how long you plan to be in the country. If only one week, this is still worthwhile if you can concentrate on one general geographical area to minimize travel and maximize the benefits of the trip. Especially if timed with a wholesaler event. There is no point in spending valuable working time crisscrossing the country on a plane. If you can allocate the time, and distribution areas or workload warrant it, two weeks can afford valuable opportunities to meet and work with distributors and host a scheduled event at each location. If, for example, a market as potentially valuable as New York has taken on your wines, it could be the right time to really concentrate on solidifying the relationship and making those important sales that will impress the distributor and encourage their support. This will not necessarily mean just Manhattan; your visit could also provide the momentum needed for upstate New York and the Burroughs. These are often neglected, but fruitful, markets where buyers will appreciate your time. The point is that you must be prepared to be flexible and listen to your importer. They presumably have a plan and are working with their distributors to take optimum advantage of your visit.

Determine which airports you will arrive and depart from. They may be at opposite ends of the country. For example, if you have an agent in British Columbia you wish to see in combination with this trip, or coordinating your trip to coincide with Vin Expo, communicate this to your importer so that flights and arrangements will be made accordingly to depart from the most convenient location and between appropriate dates. You won't want to end up in California when you need to get back to New York the next day to take a flight to Paris.

No matter what the length of your visit, please do not expect to be busy every day of the week. Everyone appreciates the expense and effort involved in your undertaking, but the simple fact is that no one works on a Sunday and you will find few distributors working on a Saturday either. The exceptions to this would be trade shows, some in-store tastings or wine dinners, although many of these will be scheduled during the week when there is greater likelihood of attendance, or less likelihood that it will interfere with high activity days of the venue. Wine dinners, advertised afternoon tastings at stores or wine bars and casual store tastings are all potentially excellent opportunities and could conceivably be on the weekend, but require a good deal of pre-trip planning and the willing cooperation of the distributor. There are also some states where tastings are not permitted by state law and restaurants where it will be difficult to schedule a wine dinner on a Saturday night, one of the busiest nights of the week. Again, this is all to inform you of the variables involved and how important planning and communication will be.

When the trip is longer, you may appreciate having a Saturday to travel from one location to the next and the Sunday to rest or see something of a city.

Budget

No one should have any preconceived notions about the asset value or income level of a winery, vineyard or brand owner. Quite often an enterprise is not yet self-sufficient and budget must be carefully considered. I know a vineyard owner who has been plowing money into his venture for at least five years now, not yet having seen a profit. His vines were young and his wines, although still good, have reflected a certain lack of ripeness and finesse. Finally, this year he expects to make sufficient sales to turn a profit. His uphill battle, and long term goals, are not unique, so although there are certain expectations, which I'll outline, there will hopefully not be any lavish spending expectations of you as you embark on a U.S. market visit. Plans should be made according to *your* budget and a commonsense approach to marketing your wines as a profitable undertaking.

With that in mind, consider the following:

- **Hotels**

    Manhattan, New York is clearly going to be more expensive than Dayton, Ohio.

- **Airfare**

    Across country is more expensive than in-state, booking in advance less expensive than last minute.

- **Local transportation**

    Will you have to take taxis everywhere or ride the train from another state, or do you need to rent a car? Are salespeople, brokers or distributor representatives able to pick you up in most instances?

- **Cost of shipping wine**

    Hopefully your wine is already available from your importer and the distributors with whom you will meet. Shipping new vintages air freight from your home country in anticipation of sales is an expensive, and possibly risky, enterprise.

- **Expectations of the distributor in that area**

  Whether, for example, they expect you to take the sales team to dinner or lunch, provide bottles for sales calls around the trade show or stay several days to work the market.

- **Tie-in with other markets**

  If you rent a car to drive from one area in close proximity to another, or make a quick flight to an adjacent city or state to work that market or attend their trade show this tie-in will provide some economic advantage.

In evaluating any other marketing you might be asked to do in conjunction with the trip or a show, the considerations are not only whether you can afford it, but whether it will result in a meaningful return.

Paving the Way

It may appear to be not only courteous, but appropriate, for your importer to accompany you to each location to pave the way, introduce you to the distributor principals and make this a smoother trip in a foreign country. In fact, it sounds like absolutely the right thing to do! But unfortunately, unless the importer has a healthy budget and the trip is also going to dovetail with their own sales trips, the reality is that it is far more practical for you to embark on the itinerary that has been set out for you, and not incur additional expenses in duplicating the effort by involving your importer. Their time may well be best spent monitoring your trip from home base, and making adjustments or communicating to principals in advance of your arrival. Meeting your importer at a prearranged point, especially if a trade show is involved, or starting or ending your trip at your importer's location to discuss business or see some accounts would be essential, but for them to accompany you on every leg across the country is usually impractical.

To someone unfamiliar with this vast country, it may seem daunting at first to set out alone. But the experienced, or even the well-organized new importer will have arranged for every contingency, including which airports you arrive at and depart from, what mode of transportation you will be using, whether someone can or cannot pick you up, the hotels, contact details for all persons with whom you will be working and arrangements for functions. Most salespeople will be more than willing to pick you up at your hotel for the day's sales calls.

Alternatively, there are perhaps brokers and regional managers or brand ambassadors at various locations around the country who will act as the local host. It will depend upon the resources or size of your importer's business, so I would prefer that you are prepared for different scenarios. They can all work, as long as sufficient preparation has been made and monitoring is in place.

Importers have various ways to approach the supplier trip. Their approach will often depend on how long the trip will be and of course other factors related to events, general planning and commitments. Some importers will travel to each new city and attend each meeting with you. This is especially feasible when the territory is manageable in terms of size and travel budget. Perhaps an area that can be navigated by car, perhaps one state or two or three smaller states. It is an opportunity for you to get to know one another better and discuss strategy and topics that are easier to talk through in person. A state as extensive, diverse and populous as California may take up the bulk of your wine, in which case your importer is more likely to accompany you, since most of the trip can be accomplished by driving or short plane rides.

Larger, but less densely populated geographical regions, where flight arrangements are necessary and often expensive, become more problematic. This can be handled either by you, in conjunction with your importer's plans of course, or by the importer with your authority. Usually, the supplier makes their own arrangements, if necessary organizing a discounted multi-ticket fare. The importer often makes the accommodation bookings because there are so many considerations in each city—proximity to distributor's office or event, quality and value of hotel, ease of pick up by sales person and so on. But the choice is entirely up to you, having regard to budget and requirements.

The meshing of personalities and work styles becomes quite important when traveling together on the road in the pursuit of sales. The most significant relationship will be with your importer, but brand managers, distributor sales reps, brokers and whoever is working closely with you during your visit will ultimately impact sales. The purpose of your visit is obviously to sell wine, but this can most easily be accomplished when the sales rep enjoys working with your wine, or the brand manager sees you as someone whose wines he'd like to promote within their portfolio. Never underestimate the positive, and negative, effect your approach can have on your wines.

Trip Protocol
There is a protocol to consider with every interaction and meeting along the way. Perhaps it will seem I go into excessive detail on this aspect, depending upon your degree of familiarity with doing business here or your own level of intuitive professionalism, but cultural differences prevail across the world and many styles that work where you call home may not necessarily be acceptable in the U.S.

If this is a wine brand representative's first trip, I have always tried to prepare them for expectations regarding the sales call and their particular presentation. It is important to be aware of what to expect in a typical "ride-along" day with a sales rep—and especially what might constitute a good day—who pays for lunch, a rundown of tipping in the U.S. and a general overview of the markets you will be visiting. Without wanting to appear condescending, I have found it necessary to prepare a supplier for an account presentation in the areas of diplomacy and expectations. Buyers, who have to endure a constant parade of salespeople throughout their day, often have short attention spans and short fuses and it is very easy to overstay your welcome or inadvertently insult the buyer. These are some brief examples, with more explanation later:

- Having the direct winery supplier visit the store is normally a unique and welcome opportunity for buyers to pick their brains on a region, ask esoteric questions and generally add to the store of information. However, they do not want to be lectured or talked down to. They do not always want to be given tons of technical information and have the winery owner talk in explicit detail about their vineyard and techniques, although some do. I once followed an appointment by a brand owner who apparently owned a fabulous château somewhere in Europe. He spent his own and the buyer's valuable time talking about his estate, not the wine, and displaying 8x10 photographs of this magnificent palace. As this particular story was related to me by the irritated retail store buyer, he declined to buy the products of the château owner "because *he* obviously doesn't need the money and I know other suppliers who do." In the same way I would advise an importer or other wine professional, a winery owner will benefit by being sensitive to the situation, the personalities and the receptivity of their audience.

- The last thing a potential buyer for a wine wants to hear is how much better this particular wine is than anything else they have in the store. They don't want to have their current selection ridiculed or denigrated, nor be the recipient of negative gossip about a certain vineyard's practices, whose wines they happen to have prominently displayed in a case stack or end cap. However superior you feel your wine may be to others in the market, and it may well be, remember you are insulting not only the buyer's own palate but potentially all Americans!

As an importer, I would always give the distributor (i.e. brand manager, sales manager, owner, etc.) a synopsis of the supplier's own expectations in regards to their market and an overview of the individual's personality in the hope that this allows the distributor to mesh and accommodate personalities and expectations in the field, that is, choice of salesperson, accounts, timetable and other considerations. This is all in the pursuit of a better outcome for all involved. I'm not necessarily referring to quirks and personality traits. It might simply mean that this winemaker likes to work long hours and would really appreciate having evening events scheduled as much as possible, in addition to the "work-withs" during daytime. It may be that they have never been to the U.S. before, so it may take them a little time to acclimate, but they are excited about the prospect of helping with sales, or it may be that while English is not their first language, they speak it fluently.

Defining Expectations
Although buyers may sometimes be terse and impatient, most people will be especially polite to you as you make your way through on-premise (restaurant) and off-premise (retail) accounts, out of respect for your role and the distance you have come to see the account. The buyer may also, in a misguided attempt to be complimentary to a wine brand principal, tell you how much they love the wines and suggest that they will be purchased just as soon as they can find room in their inventory, on the floor or on their wine list. I don't mean to sound cynical, but this may or may not be true. However, to the uninitiated winery owner, this is a sign that everywhere they go people love and buy their wines. I believe it is far more useful to hear how your wines are perceived, either positively or negatively as a result of market forces, competition or the wine's own characteristics, and I encourage you to ask for honest feedback. Empty promises don't sell wine and don't help you understand the market or make adjustments in areas such as planting, production or allocation. And hearing only positive feedback isn't doing your importer any favors either. In time, as a result of your diligent and consistent efforts, the wines will speak for themselves.

* * *

Final Thoughts

It is the pre-trip preparation that becomes vital as you proceed on the actual trip. Once you have flown to the U.S. and are on the road, traveling from city to city, it is too late to start planning events, meetings and tastings. These should all have been in place months ago. The trip is to bring your stage of the planning and preparation to fruition as part of a team. Trips are a welcome adjunct and even essential element, but management of this market and the bulk of the U.S. sales will still rest with your importer. An appreciation of the appropriate number and duration of market visits, awareness of the nuances of cultural approach and listening to the market's response will always serve you well in the long run and the resulting trips will become productive exercises for you.

Part of the planning is obviously to understand expectations and what your importer has arranged for you beforehand. I imported the wines of one winemaker/owner who put all his energies into establishing his brand as a benchmark for the styles and varietals he made on the world stage. As part of this process, he had determined that he was also of such importance that he had to be treated with great respect when he visited the United States and would only agree to certain functions, befitting his stature. I received a frantic call from his office, in his country of origin, saying the winemaker/owner was refusing to budge from the airport in Virginia until someone came to pick him up. I was in California at the time, so it certainly wasn't going to be me, but I placed a call to the local distributor and they informed me that they had already told him that there was no one available to pick him up and they requested that the supplier take a taxi to his hotel. He was not due to work with anyone until the next morning anyway, and taking a taxi from the airport to the hotel should have been an easy matter for him. Unfortunately, the supplier's stubbornness on this point unnecessarily cost him the goodwill of the distributor. And when you've lost the goodwill of your distributor you've also lost sales, something he could not afford to do at this stage of his business trajectory.

Another winemaker, who had become something of a celebrity and whose wines were met with great acclaim in the U.S., was also a diva, so that the sales manager and I lived in a constant state of dread while he was in the country. He was always sleeping in and missing flights, exhibiting outrageous behavior, turning up to events late or ignoring the guests. Although his celebrity gave him an enormous edge, as it often does in this country, sales eventually suffered and he was no longer welcome in many locations.

Another winery owner and his wife brought their newborn baby on account visits and to events, openly breastfeeding the infant during discussions, to the shock of their hosts. This led to distracted appointments, which resulted in an overall lack of focus and an inability to maximize significant sales opportunities.

These market visits are too important, and too expensive to all concerned, to leave to chance and should be approached with appropriate professionalism. The examples I used are clearly extremes, but they did happen, along with many other different examples of poorly executed sales trips. If you are in doubt, ask your importer. If you have a specific request, ask your importer. Based on their knowledge of their customers and their needs, they will be sure to accommodate you if they can, but equally sure to tell you when they cannot.

As for the purpose of your trip, always remember it is to increase sales. Your support of this market will be greatly appreciated, but don't forget that the importer has his or her ear to the ground on a daily basis. Maintaining objectivity about your wines, with the understanding that every country has distinctive perceptions, will allow your importer to guide you. Instead of asking your importer, *so why haven't you sold more?* when your wines are greeted with enthusiastic praise by a retailer, the question should be *so how can **we** sell more?*

13

On the Road

Every market visit is different in terms of the scope and makeup of the days you spend with each sales rep. A usual time span in each individual distributor's area would be two to three days, perhaps coordinated by you with a trip to a contiguous market, so that you may have two days in Nevada and two days in Arizona, for example. Remember that the wholesaler/distributor may only be licensed in their own state, but if their coverage area is quite vast and not easily drivable, they may ask you to spend a day or two each in several cities over the span of a week. I have felt a bit like a relay baton on occasion as I have worked a city or county and been driven an hour to the next destination where another salesperson picks me up and so on throughout a week, but it has been a very effective way to cover their regions. I have also rented a car and driven myself, or taken a flight between cities if the distance has been too great, such as in Texas, or taken a train between Washington DC and New York. It is one way to get to know the U.S. as well, and the way each market relates to or differs from another.

Protocol

Your time may consist of a day of restaurant and retail accounts, sometimes only one or the other if the sales rep specializes in off-premise (retail stores) or on-premise (restaurants). Either way, we hope the person has been sufficiently interested and organized to plan a solid day of worthwhile appointments for you. This is not a time for ego massaging, where the sales rep takes you to what are often called the "milk run" accounts that already have your product or where the salesperson can easily get your wines in on his or her own. You should welcome the challenging accounts, the new restaurant or difficult retailer where you have the opportunity to assist with a placement that the salesperson has not had any luck making. This not only creates additional sales for his or her territory, but should engender good will and contribute to their enthusiasm for you and your wines. I believe there is never a better opportunity to make a sale than when the "face" of the brand is visiting the account. There can be no more knowledgeable or passionate ambassador.

On the other hand, there may be special accounts they take you to, where they are on very good terms with the buyer and have fostered a relationship that produces large and regular sales, even without your assistance. Undertaken in the right way, this is an opportunity for the sales rep to tacitly signify to the retailer that they (the retailer) are important and, as a mark of respect, have brought the direct representative of the wine (you) to meet them. The retailer, if they are already familiar with your wine and carry it, can now identify with the brand and ask questions and obtain more information about the wines. You will be able to bring the vineyard alive for them and can provide intimate details about the region, viticulture, winemaking techniques and other items of interest. It is the chance to tell them why this particular red wine has a higher percentage of Viognier than most Rhône blends, what the vintage was like that year, or what measures the vineyard takes to be truly considered biodynamic. I don't mean to be too repetitious, but it is still advisable to rein in your enthusiasm for your subject somewhat and remember you are there to sell your wine, so be mindful of their time and listen to your customer's needs.

The salesperson, by taking you to this account, has also demonstrated a desire to promote your wines and become an ambassador for your brand. They could, after all, bring almost any supplier to this account if the relationship they enjoy with the account buyer is a unique one. They have determined that you and your wines are worth this placement.

The *minimum* day should comprise approximately six to eight appointments, starting around 10am and finishing at around 6pm, with a short lunch break. Regional variations can result in greater distances covered between accounts in a salesperson's territory, or longer waits at accounts can reduce the number you can fit into the day, but this is a general rule of thumb. Although lunch may be scheduled as an appointment, during which wines are poured for the sommelier, more usually there will be little opportunity for lunch, especially when you are working with the best salespeople. It may appear less cultured than what you are accustomed to in Europe or South America, for example, but there is no leisurely midday dining experience if it doesn't serve a business purpose, unless the salesperson is unmotivated or unable to find sufficient accounts.

There are many other constructs to a day, including a scenario that could start, for example, at 8am when you are picked up at your hotel and driven two hours to the first account, and ending at 11pm when you finish the scheduled wine dinner. It is an exhausting kind of day, but I have done variations on it often and I endure whatever hours and program put in place for me, knowing that I am getting the most out of this trip. I also respect the willingness of the distributor and the salesperson to put this much effort and time into making the trip successful.

Although as an importer I have driven a rental car to meet reps at out of the way places, I would expect that most often you will be picked up at your hotel and will not need a car. You are not expected to be familiar with driving in the U.S., but if a region cannot be navigated without renting a car between stops and you do not feel comfortable driving, make sure you have advised your importer prior to the trip so that other arrangements can be made.

Local Customs

It goes without saying that customs differ from country to country and I have been told by some producers that as the guest in the U.S. they initially expected to be "hosted" in terms of having their meals paid for, just as they might entertain guests at their home, winery restaurant or local village bistro. I do understand this reasoning but, when on the road in the U.S., it is customary, and universally expected, that you will pay for the sales rep's lunch. The sales rep is usually working on commission and has committed a day to showing and selling your wines. They have foregone other opportunities and wines in order to focus solely on yours.

During the course of the day, the dedicated professional has either planned the selling opportunity lunch for you, or will make a brief and relatively inexpensive stop to refuel and be back on the street. Beware the sales rep who brings you to an expensive restaurant for an extended lunch period, where they only stock Californian wines and will never consider representing yours. This is the opportunistic sales rep who is looking, literally, for the free lunch, and once you leave there is very little post-visit sales activity. I have been far more impressed with the rep who had me begging for sustenance at 4pm because I was lightheaded from hunger and, in their zeal to see more accounts, they had forgotten to stop.

If you are with your importer and the distributor principal has invited you both for lunch or dinner to discuss future business or chart the course of your new distribution with them, there are no hard and fast rules on who picks up the check. It will depend upon the situation and the inclination of all parties involved.

The customary number of wines to take out on sales calls is six to eight. This will depend of course on how many wines are in your brand. If you have four wines, all readily available for this market, then four wines are all that will be shown. However, if you are only showing two, it is possible there will be some overlap in the distributor portfolio with another brand or supplier, which the rep will explain to you beforehand. It is hard to show only one or two wines at an appointment that may, for example, have taken a month to make. Conversely, if you have a brand with several tiers and price points, with some estate-grown labels, some negociants and so on, tailor the day to the wines that need the most attention. Too many wines will be off-putting to the buyers, who know a large number will take a long time to taste through. However, there are sales people who may decide to pull several more from inventory, keep them cool and secure in the car and have available to the accounts the wines they feel may best suit their palates or needs. In my opinion, this is a perfectly acceptable way to conduct the day.

Please note, the importer will most likely be invoiced for 100% of the samples used during these 'work-withs' or 'ride-withs' in charges called 'bill-backs', but will also potentially benefit from the greater diversity of opportunity, as long as the samples are used to best advantage. In other words, opening twelve wines of which three to four may be poured for most accounts will result in a lot of leftover wine. In this case, advance planning by the sales rep will result in gathering potential customers to taste at a restaurant at lunch, utilizing the wines at dinner or another tasting that night, or making sure they are properly sealed and gassed for use the next day on the salesperson's regular route. In some instances, you could also work with these opened samples yourself during the next day's work-with, but since you're only there on rare occasions you will most likely want to show the wines at optimum quality, newly opened. Of course, some big reds will benefit from aeration and fortified wines will be fine.

In terms of other expenses incurred during the day, a distributor salesperson will usually be reimbursed by their distributor for fuel for the car, subway tokens, taxi fares and parking.

Outreach

Cultivate distributor sales staff if you want them to remember your wine, take it under their wings and nurture its growth in their market. This can be accomplished by asking the distributor or importer to identify the best salespeople or by developing a relationship with whomever has been assigned to you and getting them excited about the wines and your region. However, bigger and faster impact commonly requires scheduling a presentation for a Friday morning sales meeting. This is the traditional team meeting held once a week or once a month, depending upon the wholesaler, and while part of it is devoted to the distributor's own business and housekeeping matters—quotas, reports, problems, etc.—a portion of the time is typically allocated to suppliers who wish to come in and promote their brands. I'd like to offer my suggestions for getting the most out of this meeting. These suggestions may sound a little blunt, but I am always intent on providing you with information that is going to place you in the most advantageous position:

- First of all, please make your presentation interesting and keep them awake. These poor people have frequently been subjected to boring presentations with the same tired product, or overly technical discourses delivered in a monotone. This is their time you are monopolizing. They could be putting it to better use and, furthermore, will do so as soon as you release them if you haven't made your talk motivating, intriguing, fun and/or potentially financially attractive. Use Power Point if the time allows and it enhances your presentation, but it is by no means necessary and not always an improvement. Engaging them is paramount.

- Second, stick to the time limit. This could be five minutes or thirty, but there *will* be a stated time limit. There could be presentations before and after yours, or the salespeople have already spent part of the morning on their own in-house agenda. It is only courteous to adhere to this stipulation and will endear you to the sales team if you do.

- Bring wine for them to taste, or ensure that it is pulled from inventory and ready. Not so much that they develop palate fatigue (remember there could be others before you) but sufficient in number and diversity to reflect your signature and the region. These could comprise wines already in their book, upcoming vintages, or new wines under consideration by management. Tasting through the wines while you describe something of the vineyard, background, style and pricing allows the information to marry with the product. Very often, this may be the first opportunity they have had to taste the wines and this is the occasion you may find your brand's champion—the one who falls in love with it and whose mental wheels are turning over as to where they can place it and how they can sell it.

- Give the sales team key words to use with each wine or the brand in general—phrases that distinguish it from other wines, or makes it easier to remember. Keep it simple. Don't overload them with technical information or complicated descriptions. Consider that yours is one of many brands in their book and they cannot absorb all the information at one presentation. It could be something about the wine or grapes, such as the aromatics, age of the vines, yield or about the vineyard. Is the vineyard soil rare and contributes to the wine's unique characteristics? Is an adjacent vineyard home to a well-known producer or do you both source the same grapes? How about the vignerons themselves: third generation, same winemaker as..., previously made by.... Whatever it is, try to make your references a point of difference and not the usual descriptions they have heard a thousand times before. Keep the technology and elaborate backgrounds for the handout material or direct them to your website or your importer's website.

- Give them more reason to take out your wines. Discuss this beforehand with your importer and distributor management, but make the week you are there, or the week following your presentation, a time of monetary incentives for most sold, most placements or $xx a case program. This is not essential by any means, and I have often conducted sales seminars without it, but it is an opportunity for a tangible value-added piece of your presentation if it fits your budget. A non-tangible way to stimulate sales would be to develop a rapport with all or some of the team, so that they feel they are aiding the relative success of someone they like and respect. You would be surprised at how often a supplier can lack a relatable personality or be arrogant or insensitive. A supplier who is none of these is in a far better position to be favorably remembered.

- Leave them with an invitation to visit the vineyard or email you if they have questions. Their first point of contact will be the importer and most will not take you up on your invitation to visit, but it is a way to let them know that their representation of your brand matters. And who knows, you may have inspired a salesperson to sell enough wine to be welcomed warmly at your vineyard should they decide to make this trip a goal.

Events

The planning of tastings, trade and consumer events and wine dinners will fall to your importer and the wholesaler in the respective markets, but it is something of which you should be aware so that you know which questions to ask and take nothing for granted.

Wine Dinners

Wine dinners are very popular for the traveling supplier because it showcases your wine in a comfortable ambiance and in conjunction with food. You have paying attendees who will be looking forward to hearing you talk about the wines in far more knowledgeable and intimate details than they will ever hear anywhere else and they will be relaxed and receptive. However, unless selling wines in the U.S. market is a hobby for you, it must still be a productive and profitable event.

In terms of marketing, the success of a wine dinner comes down to the most practical questions—what does it cost and how does it benefit your wines. As with everything else, it has to make sense. Donating dozens of bottles and flying in for a wine dinner without measurable financial gain is just throwing money away. The restaurant will appreciate the exposure and additional revenue they receive, the distributor will think you naïve and you will realize that you just wasted valuable resources.

Wine dinners should only ever be agreed to if you, and your importer, have determined one or more of the following:

1. The cost of wine to you is negligible or nil or shared equally with the restaurant and/or distributor and is reasonable.
2. There is a tie-in with a local retailer to buy the wine or the restaurant has its own adjoining wine bar/retail outlet where the wines will immediately be available for the dinner's guests.
3. Wine(s) will go on the restaurant wine list or are already there.

There is never any reason to conduct a wine dinner where you or the importer are expected to foot the wine bill in its entirety, there is no exposure for either brand or wholesaler and there is no plan for follow through.

As much as the evening's guests will enjoy the wine and food pairings, the opportunity to learn about the nuances of flavors and your scintillating banter, they will forget the name of the wine and what it looks and tastes like as soon as they don their coats and walk out the door. They don't mean to, but once the magic of the evening wears off, they are back to their lives and the wine is relegated to a pleasant experience. Unless there is the more attractive inducement of a discount at the local retailer or the retailer has brought VIP customers to the dinner for the express purpose of taking orders to be filled from the store. In states where it is legal, and more often at a private dinner rather than a public event, wines may even be sold at the dinner, slated for delivery at a later date.

At the very least, the wines have to be available in the area. There is absolutely no point making the effort to host a wine dinner when the wines are not likely to be available for a couple of months, because there is no return on investment. Unless—the usual caveat—it is an iconic, high demand brand where consumers are waiting with bated breath for the next vintage and this is a privileged insider's preview. Under that circumstance, consumers will be very familiar with the brand and feel a connection with the wines that will provide a further impetus to purchase them when available.

Determine how many different wines will be served, the anticipated quantity of total bottles, how many people are expected and the number of courses. If you don't have a dessert wine, a Cabernet or Merlot may take its place with chocolate or cheese, but often the chef or restaurant owner would prefer to have a true dessert wine to expand the choices and finish the meal with flair. As an importer, I have willingly agreed to the inclusion of something such as a botrytis wine, Port, Muscat or Tokay from another portfolio if I have not represented one at the time, but a description of the dessert pairing should be simply added as an addendum to your presentation, not with equal focus. A mix of suppliers at the same dinner should definitely be avoided and will normally result in diluting your event and your presentation.

Quite often, the wine dinner is scheduled several months in advance, in which case vintages may have changed or wines are expected to be shipped just prior to the dinner. Be sure to follow up with your importer and verify the correct wines and their availability.

I have no doubt that you are familiar with food and wine pairings and probably have conducted many wine dinners over the course of your involvement with wine, but I still make no assumptions on cultural familiarity. You can absorb or discard whatever you wish of the following suggestions, based on your own experience and what has worked for you. The advice about speaking at wine dinners is a little like that for the sales staff Friday tastings: keep it interesting, entertaining and to a time limit. The audience is very different from the sales meeting, of course, and the information you impart is tailored for the consumer, but the point is to give them a memorable experience that also translates into sales.

Formats for wine dinners can be varied, but usually there is a reception wine given to the guests upon arrival, in a cocktail pre-dinner setting in a private room or part of the restaurant set aside for the dinner, giving sufficient time for everyone to arrive. This is often the time when the host speaker—importer, winemaker, winery owner, broker, export manager or national sales director, for example—can circulate, be introduced and answer questions about this first wine. The cocktail hour is an informal part of the evening and not usually conducive to public speaking.

Once the guests are seated and the first course is served, along with one to three wines chosen to pair with the food, this may be an appropriate time for you to get up and speak about the reception wine and the first course wines. This is when you might like to set the scene with background on the region and the winery and perhaps recount a funny or endearing personal story. Then it's time to launch into a brief description of each wine and its compatibility with the course. It is an opportunity to give limited technical information: the difference between French and American oak, what malolactic fermentation means (in its basic sense) are examples of what guests might find informative. Discussing a particular varietal and its role in blends, if that is part of the tasting selection, is appreciated. Do not delve into technical discussions regarding the entire process of grape to wine, unless you have been advised beforehand that this is a handpicked audience of sommeliers, for example. Otherwise, you will observe eyes glaze over and it will all be for naught. They are at the wine dinner first and foremost to enjoy good wine, appetizing food and have fun. In the process they are hoping to make discoveries and feel uniquely connected to the winery.

As each course is served, gauge the most opportune moment to get up again and talk about the wines. Keep the time reasonably short, but also consider your audience. They may be a particularly educated group who is looking forward to more technical information or background on the vineyard. Adapting your talk to the mood and atmosphere will make it a more enjoyable occasion for them. If you can see they are relaxed and having fun, be relaxed and have fun with them. Circulating during the meal, chatting with guests and inviting questions is always welcome and can often provide you with useful feedback. And of course, leave the selling up to your host.

Trade Tastings

If you have been growing grapes and making wine or overseeing a vineyard operation for some time, you will most likely be very familiar with all mode of trade tastings, from government sponsored occasions to private affairs, and many others, as discussed early on in this book. In this chapter, I am focusing primarily on events that your importer has evaluated and vetted for you. This subject should be divided into two very distinct areas: trade tastings and consumer tastings. Despite the seemingly related format, they have very little relation to one another in terms of audience and focus.

Trade Show—Distributor

In my opinion, the most important trade tasting is the one you do at the behest of a distributor appointed by your importer and one already carrying at least one of your wines. Not because this necessarily produces the best results and the most noteworthy sales—although it can—but because it demonstrates loyalty to the wholesaler and a willingness to support them in their home market efforts. It is a show organized by your importer's distributor in a specific state, where they are showcasing their entire portfolio and have invited their customers—the retail trade—to taste through this year's or this season's offerings. It can be one event in a major city where a radius of accounts is invited, or it can be a road show of sorts, held in two or three cities or regions, to take advantage of the diversity of geography, for instance resort clientele vs. urban environment, or make allowances for distances to reach the event. In addition to direct sales, it is an opportunity to meet or cement relationships with principals and sales staff, and learn more about the trade in that area.

Expenses for these events normally accrue to the importer, but these can be shared opportunities as well. Costs, organization and logistics can vary, but the desired result for the distributor—to sell the wines they represent—is your goal, so this can be a very worthwhile event. Expenses may or may not include:

- Charging for the booth or table
- Providing a table or section for free
- Having the importer provide the wine
- Sharing the cost of the wine

- Requiring a certain number of bottles
- Optional wine selections
- Requiring that all wine be pulled from the distributor's stock
- Allowing you to bring new vintages or special cuvees
- Prohibiting any wines that are not already in their inventory

As you can see, there are variables across the spectrum. Whatever the conditions the particular distributor imposes, they must be respected. They have most likely gone to a great deal of trouble to put an annual event together, renting space, providing food, printing booklets, dealing with the logistics of wine and people placement, inviting their top accounts and ensuring it is as successful as possible. Everyone's needs are important and everyone has the same agenda—to sell wine.

Each venue will be different. I have done trade tastings in the grand ballrooms of fine hotels, a zoo in Phoenix, art galleries, embassies in Washington DC, meeting rooms of moderate chain hotels, tents at the base of a waterfall in Colorado, under canopies in spacious gardens, Soho loft space in Manhattan, an Art Deco theatre in Atlanta and at the distributor's own warehouse. Budget constraints and expected attendance will often dictate the location, but the motivation is always to offer a venue and wine selection that will entice the retailer, restaurateur and occasional VIP

Figure 19 **Trade wine tasting**

customer to come to the event, or choose this one over another at the same time across town.

If this is a distributor trade event, it will also be attended by your importer. Making an appearance, supporting the distributor and assisting with sales is of equal importance to them. It will be ideal scheduling for you to work closely with your importer, and still focus on your own wines and be the expert. This will enhance what the importer is doing, even if they have other wines at the event. Aside from the practical sales aspect, you will also have an opportunity to observe your U.S. representative as they interact with distributor management, sales team and potential customers. Do they have a good rapport? Are they sure to include you in new introductions? If this is their first time in this city, are they comfortable with establishing a connection and conveying the right tone? Are they maximizing opportunities for trade placements for your wines with attendees?

Trade Show—Independent

These are a little trickier and I would never recommend signing up for this type of trade event on your own, but if this is a joint effort for your appellation, province or state, for example, it may be something your importer feels will give all brands of that region a boost, including yours.

Once again, evaluate the cost-benefit:

- Is this likely to attract the right mix or number of trade potentials?
- Is your importer looking for a distributor in the state or territory in which it is held?
- Is the cost for the table/booth reasonable?
- Does this conflict with anything your importer's distributor is already doing?
- How well organized is it?
- What is the trade-consumer ratio?
- Are there seminars?
- What is your competition?
- Is there a theme?
- Where is the venue?
- How will it be promoted?

The better organized, more appealing and well publicized the event, the greater the probability it will attract the right numbers and quality of trade. Making sure not to conflict with other, equally tempting, events in the same city, or having a series of timely seminars throughout the course of the afternoon, will also increase the attraction.

These events will invariably include a consumer component, either during or after the trade segment. Including them, at a fee, often helps organizers defray costs, raise funds for a designated cause or allow them to rent a more glamorous venue. Whatever the number of attendees or ratio of trade to consumer, when you commit to the event you commit to the consumer component. It is considered really bad form to pack up and go home after the trade component is over. Consumers have an expectation that their event fee includes a certain number of wineries or wines, or they might even be looking for your wines in particular, having read about them in the press release beforehand.

Tastings of this type are often submitted to the press, which could result in more exposure for your brand, either in being interviewed for a podcast or having your wines recommended in the food and wine section of the newspaper.

Results

You haven't come all this way, and worked this hard, to go home as if you've just been on holiday. It is reasonable for you to expect to learn the outcome of your activities at some point after your return home.

- Was there a sales spike?
- Which wines stood out?
- Which wine(s) exceeded expectations in sales?
- Which wines, if any, didn't seem to work?
- What was other feedback—positive or negative?
- Were there constructive suggestions—pricing, style, packaging, for example?
- Were there new placements?
- Did your presence make a difference?

Beyond that, what is the quantifiable result of your efforts? Certainly, you can expect to have in-depth discussions with your importer, possibly at a meeting following your last trade show together or back at the importer's office before you leave the country, where you can review each market. But you won't really have a realistic assessment of the outcome until accounts have placed their orders, sometimes at a much later date, and the incentive programs (if any) have produced the desired effect.

Now is the time to determine if you need to make adjustments to your U.S. market projections, or to establish a course of action on new wines, based on feedback and after discussion with your importer. To that end, it will be helpful to have access to depletion reports that we hope the distributors will give to your importer.

Placement Reports

This refers to the account placements made by the distributor and specifies which wine and vintage is placed at what account in their region. It can be a difficult report to obtain from some wholesalers, especially on a regular basis. The time it takes to prepare is time they may not wish to devote to something that has no discernible value for them. Occasionally, wholesalers are reluctant to divulge what they consider proprietary information they fear may be passed along to their replacement in the future. However, most have computer programs that readily allow them to produce these reports and should have no problem supplying the information. It can be useful to tie your incentive programs to these quantifiable placements, and in the case of restaurant glass pour programs is essential. Knowledge of where your wines are placed in the market can assist your importer with their ability to target accounts and stimulate sales.

The reluctance some distributors have about divulging the specifics of all their placements can be well founded, but this should not be their first concern. If they are performing well to reasonable expectations, and honoring their financial commitments, there should be no reason for your importer to consider taking your brand elsewhere.

AUGUST, 2014					PLACEMENT REPORT NEW YORK DISTRIBUTOR			BLUESTONE WINE SOLUTIONS		
INV NO	INV-DATE	ACCT#	ACCOUNT NAME	ITEM-NO	PRODUCT DESCRIPTION		VINT	SIZE	CASE!	BTLS
0862583	08/12/2014	41593	THE MEETING HOUSE	58601NV1	CHAPEL HILL PARSONS NOSE SHIRAZ		2012	12/750	2	0
0863271	08/17/2014	NJ6697	LANDRY'S RESTAURANT	58603081	CHAPEL HILL BUSH VINE GRENACHE		2011	12/750	0	6
0861506	08/08/2014	23540	MR WRIGHT'S FINE WINE	78900061	KEIST WINES CEPAGE		2011	12/750	12	0
0863271	08/17/2014	NJ6697	LANDRY'S RESTAURANT	78900062	WILLIAM WHITE RESERVE CABERNET		2013	12/750	2	3
0864231	08/23/2014	01880	AQUAGRILL	78900073	WILLIAM WHITE RESERVE CHARDONNAY		2012	12/750	4	0
0864781	08/25/2014	36585	PASANELLA & SON VINTNERS	78900083	HAZY BLUR SHIRAZ KANGAROO ISLD		2010	12/750	4	0
0861614	08/09/2014	27036	BEEKMAN STREET BISTRO	78901064	HAZY BLUR CAB KANGAROO ISLD		2010	12/750	2	0

Figure 20 Placement report

Depletion Reports

Incentive programs should be tied to depletions—in other words, the depletion of their inventory by means of sales. Otherwise, there is no "incentive" for the distributor to produce records to back up the program. The programming you and your importer may have put in place should hold the distributor accountable to the extent that programming money is not paid until a depletion report shows the cases sold that month or quarter. This is a basic and good reason for depletion reports, but there is more.

It's really in a supplier's best interests to see how well the distributor is performing with a brand overall. It allows you and your importer to see the pace of sales, determine an order point, determine where they may require some assistance to move a wine faster and anticipate container shipments. Hopefully, this information indicates progress. Unfortunately, in some instances, what the depletions indicate are that your wines are moving at glacial speed and at this rate you will be three vintages ahead before they are ready for the next order. If this is the case, another order is unlikely anyway. But if your importer can catch this trend soon enough, there is a greater likelihood of reversing it. A call to the wholesaler to see if it is a problem that may be addressed is the first order of business for your importer. If the issue lies with how your wines fit in their market, or lack of interest from their sales team, better that you both know than to remain in ignorant bliss until it's too late. It provides a timely opening for your importer to explore other prospects in the market.

INVENTORY DEPLETION REPORT

NEW YORK DISTRIBUTOR

BLU05001 PLC: 100 - Last Supplier: BLUESTONE Sales Period: 08/01/2014 - 08/31/2014 Start Inventory: 07/29/2014 End Inventory: 08/31/2014

Sequence by: SUPPLIER

Item No.	*Product Description*	*Vint*	*Packin*	*PLC*	*Starting*		*Purchases*		*Adjustments*		*Sales NY*		*Sales NJ*		*Ending Inv*	
					Cas	*Btls*	*Ca*	*Btls*	*Cas*	*Btls*	*Cases*	*Btls*	*Cas*	*Btls*	*Cas*	*Btls*
BWS - BLUESTONE WINE SOLUTIONS LLC																
58501081	CHAPEL HILL PARSONS NOSE SHIRAZ	2012	12/750	CPL	0	0	7	0	0	0	3	0	0	0	4	0
58502081	CHAPEL HILL BUSH VINE GRENACHE	2011	12/750	CPL	0	0	4	0	0	0	0	0	0	0	4	0
58601NV1	KEST WINES CEPAGE	2011	12/750	KST	0	0	13	11	0	0	3	2	0	0	10	9
58602081	WILLIAM WHITE RESERVE CHARDONNAY	2013	12/750	WWR	0	0	4	0	0	0	0	0	0	0	4	0
58603061	WILLIAM WHITE RESERVE CABERNET SAUVIGNON	2012	12/750	WWR	0	0	4	0	0	0	0	0	0	3	3	3
78900061	BLUE BYRENEES SPARKLING SHIRAZ	NV	12/750	BPS	6	10	7	0	0	0	10	3	0	3	3	4
78901071	HAZY BLUR SHIRAZ KANGAROO ISLD	2010	12/750	HZB	3	9	4	0	0	0	1	1	0	0	6	6
78902061	HAZY BLUR CAB KANGAROO ISLAND	2010	12/750	HZB	7	11	0	0	0	0	0	3	0	0	7	8
					16	30	43	11	0	0	17	9	[illegible]	6	42	32

Figure 21 **New York distributor depletions**

* * *

Final Thoughts

I have so many stories from my time on the road but I will never forget one winery owner whose wines were extremely good but who lacked any warmth in his public personality and had a difficult time connecting to the customer. At one retail store, he was asked by the store owner why he had chosen this Chardonnay for the U.S. market, knowing that there were two or three others in the brand lineup. To my great discomfort, the answer from the winery owner was, "because the American palate is not sophisticated enough to appreciate my better wines." Although the store owner remained cordial and courteous, it was evident to me that he felt insulted and I knew our time there was wasted. Needless to say, no sale was made at this account. This winery owner not only lacked warmth but a basic understanding of the American consumer and made his own misinformed assumptions.

There are many more affable, courteous and well-mannered suppliers visiting the country representing their wines, but it is the badly behaving ones that become noticed and their stories are repeated across the industry.

Dynamic personalities can be captivating and memorable. One winery owner I knew was making a large retail store appearance and with his booming voice, funny stories and contagious personality he drew customers to him. He signed bottles, told jokes and actually placed the bottles into charmed customer's carts. At the time, it was one of the more successful events the store had ever hosted.

However, when dynamism tips over into manic and offensive behavior, it becomes problematic. There are those who enjoy seeing a well-known winemaker's branded, naked backside and others who are aghast. People will forgive a so-called celebrity a great deal, but if you don't want to be embarrassed to see yourself on the Internet or have the conversation revolve around your antics rather than your wine, consider the consequences of your actions.

No one expects faultless demeanor, but attention to the purpose of your visit and respect for the host or your customers is an important step towards cementing those critical relationships. It is you who will benefit most of all.

14

Thinking Outside the Box

In the beginning of your quest, as you were struggling to find a point of entry to the U.S. market, it was all about finding an importer with adequate funds and the ability to purchase your wine and give you distribution in the U.S. After that, I'm assuming by what I've been told by so many that you weren't quite sure what your role was except to make sure that the importer—or distributor, agent, broker or whatever you originally thought this title to be—ordered your wine with such frequency that it allowed you to turn your attention to other matters, such as your vineyard management or new markets. However, as you have learned thus far, it is a very different proposition to achieve successful wines sales in the U.S. Success defined as ongoing purchases that meet your expectations for growth and that are paid as agreed. The U.S. market is arguably one of the most important in the world, but to succeed in it requires constant vigilance and a collaborative partnership with your customer, the importer. The importer partner working within the three-tier system is the conventional and usually the best prospect for most brands and one that is the easiest to manage. There are other options you might consider, with opportunities that vary depending upon the brand, price, volume and your own needs. As I've said, the three-tier system does still apply in these scenarios, but they widen the opening to opportunity.

Retail Chains

This term encompasses a range of operations:

- Multi-unit, family-owned retail stores in one county
- Huge, warehouse style chain across the state
- Grocery stores across one state, or several states
- Statewide restaurant chain, or restaurant chain in fifteen states
- National retail store chain with centralized buyer
- Specialty stores with an emphasis on organic or kosher, by either region or state
- Regional contract with a national club chain for limited placement
- National contract with the same club chain for floor stacking of high volume wines

The nature of these businesses and the approach you take will vary dramatically from one to another. Much will depend upon your wines as well. I would not attempt to mislead you into thinking the retail chain route would be an easy one, but it can often be the most lucrative and sometimes the only point of entry into this country. Above all, research and dedication are required to uncover, for example:

- Whether your wines are suited to a particular chain
- If price points, packaging, features, volume and styles are consistent with their focus
- If you have sufficient volume for their needs
- If their buyer is at a centralized location or whether they have regional buyers, or both
- If regional, whether this can be an opportunity to build your brand to attract the national buyer
- What you understand about the approach that must be taken to attract the interest of the buyer and move the process forward
- The expensive and onerous requirements of a chain in exchange for national placement, such as marketing and personnel support

- What other expectations they may have of their supplier, such as whether they require private labels, specific pricing, an exacting delivery schedule, sourcing of other wines or label changes as their needs change
- Whether they only use experienced chain brokers to pitch wines to them (which you can find, but you must know this first)
- Whether they require you to have distributors in place *first*; in other words, you have secured wholesaler partners in the regions or states in which their stores are located, who are in a position to support your margins and delivery needs. This can be achieved after demonstrable interest from the chain, but it must be quantifiable interest, such as an actual purchase order or contract with the retailer. No distributor will consider your wines based on your statement that such-and-such chain is interested, unless they were independently considering your brand for their own distribution
- Whether your competition in that chain precludes the inclusion of your wines, because they are too similar in price, packaging and region and doing well; conversely, if your competition is not doing well because of negative price, packaging or stylistic impact, this may be your opportunity

Fortunately, the Internet makes it so much easier to do this research from a distance. All large chains, and most smaller ones, will have guidelines on their websites for wine submissions. Further exploration via email or phone can uncover who to direct your inquiries to and reveal other details, such as if there is a specific time of the year for tasting, what they're looking for and if they will deal directly with you. Much of your focus (i.e. which type of chain to pursue) and your success will depend upon your product and your production. For example (as of this writing), if you have a value-priced Prosecco or Moscato from Italy that you feel will blow the competition out of the water, it may be the perfect moment to ride that trend with well-timed approaches to chains such as Costco, Trader Joe's, Total Wine, Beverages and More, and others like them with large enough buying power to be able to purchase containers on a DI (Direct Import) basis, whether they are in one state or across the country. The larger chains like these are more likely to want to deal directly with the supplier and have the logistical resources to bring to the transaction. They have 'clearing' importers and distributors and they welcome having a direct line to the supplier. Even though this is still adhering to the three-tier system, their profit margins are greatly enhanced by being the true direct purchaser with nominal payments to the importer and wholesaler for providing access to each tier of the system. In this scenario, the importer and wholesaler, or in some cases the importer/wholesaler, has actually predicated their entire business on this model, to profit from smaller margins with larger volume and guaranteed sales.

Traditional grocery store chains will be much more difficult to penetrate, no matter what you represent, because they are heavily entrenched with chain brokers and established suppliers. They also have a culture that is markedly different from other retail operations and floor space that is prime real estate and for which a premium is paid. But that does not mean you cannot find either the right broker to approach them for you, or the right grocery buyer who may be receptive.

Of course it is not just Prosecco or Moscato, but these are obvious examples of the moment. It could be kosher, organic, well-priced French, New Zealand or Argentinean, or simply striking the right note with the buyer with a combination of product, pricing and personality. Although I have advised you somewhat differently in the case of traditional importing, if you are seriously considering the chain option and have not been to the U.S. before, or had a chance to evaluate the chains, meeting with an interested buyer would certainly be a reason to make the trip. In addition to the opportunity itself, it will be an invaluable education. Although a buyer will only meet with you if there is stated interest in your wines, or the significant potential for business, if such an opening presented itself this is definitely not an occasion to take for granted. Without connections in the U.S. or established distribution, such opportunities to break into the market this way will not come along very often. Seek out export agents in your own country who may have facilitated transactions like this before and see if they think your wines would fit this paradigm. An export broker who has dealt with DI container shipments to chains or large stores will not only have experience with what works, but will have relationships with at least one importer or a chain broker in the U.S.

Private Labels

Private labels, in this context, applies to those labels that are designed to satisfy a business opportunity or provided as an alternative label for a potential customer. Private labels allow a winery or current brand owner to introduce a *different* brand to the U.S. as an exclusive product line if they already have an existing brand in U.S. distribution. A private label can be tailored to the brand identity of the customer. Generally, it expands options for both the supplier and the U.S. wholesale or retail customer in brand distribution. Whether private labels are an option for you will obviously depend on your individual parameters. Considerations include:

- Production—sufficient to meet needs
- Varietals—whether they are of a type to appeal to current market
- Price points
- Vineyard size and capacity
- Ability to source the wines if you don't have the capacity from your own vineyard
- Consistent quantity, quality and style
- Whether you are passionate about establishing your own name brand rather than staying relatively anonymous

To some degree, the private label approach dovetails with the chain approach in that retail chains, a large box retailer or a restaurant group will be the most receptive to private labels. They often look for brands that can become a proprietary line for them, eliminating competition with other retailers, in town or on the internet. With aggressive pricing enabled by dealing directly with the producer, a retailer can offer private labels at virtually any quality level that competes favorably with even well-known brands, by offering better pricing. They won't be undercut by their rivals because no one else has this label. Responding to market trends, private labels can also deliver interchangeable varieties, or the lineup can be expanded as the brand prospers. A restaurant's markup can be comfortably generous if it knows the brand will not be found on retail shelves at any price.

If a direct approach to retailers feels right for you and private labels are an option, make this known in your initial enquiries. I cannot anticipate whether you will be successful, but it may make the difference in whether you are able to take advantage of this "outside of the box" avenue. Unless specified in a contractual agreement you have made with a customer, you could conceivably provide the same or similar wines under different private labels to buyers in other states or regions, especially if you already know the first label is selling successfully, thereby increasing your chances of anticipating the needs of the next customer.

Cruise Ships

Although some cruise lines originate or are based in foreign countries, where there may be someone with whom you can develop a relationship, all cruise lines have corporate offices in the U.S., most in California and Florida, with a few in Washington. This avenue is a bit more challenging because you also normally have to submit wines to and negotiate with U.S.-based brokers who have specific experience and trusted relationships with cruise line buyers. But opportunities to submit directly to the corporate office are still available and some even welcome submissions of new wines from the producers themselves.

To state the obvious, cruise ships are of varying sizes, go to different destinations and have a variety of themes and requirements, so part of your research should be getting to know who they are and what they might be interested in. For example, if the ship goes to an Italian port it is likely that they will want to showcase the wines of the region for their guests and if your wines are Italian this gives you an advantage. The same can be said for a themed restaurant on the ship. The ship may not go to French ports, but a French restaurant is going to want French wines on the list, at least as features. Naturally, it is not as simple as that. It takes time and an understanding of the cruise line's parameters, requiring that you submit wines for tasting and wait months for decisions, but if your wine is chosen it will be worth the wait.

Ask as many questions as possible to narrow down their requirements:

- Pricing guidelines
- Wine styles
- Label preferences
- Delivery schedules
- Release times
- Anything else that they may factor into their particular decision-making

If you are trying to get your wines on the cruise ship line's core list, be prepared for additional obstacles and a time consuming process, but if you meet their criteria then it could mean they take your whole production, or at least give you a tremendous running start on U.S. sales. For that type of placement they will require thousands of cases. Do you:

- Have sufficient production
- Have available ongoing allocation
- Understand what their initial order will be
- Know what their ongoing order quantity will be
- Have a clear picture of the length of their commitment

The advantage of core lists on cruise ships is that they often change annually to make it more interesting for the guests, which gives you an opening to pitch your wines. The flip side, however, is that because of this annual turnover, you could find yourself replaced. It is imperative, in this and any other potentially long term commitment, that you have a firm purchase order or contract so that you don't overextend yourself or increase your production in anticipation of demand that doesn't materialize.

Some cruise ships include wines for their guests in their cruise price package, but most don't and there will always be reserve and more limited-production wines available for a range of palates and budgets. Some ships cater to a wealthier clientele by virtue of the price and length of the cruise and they are looking for wines that fall into this category. Would your wines be considered of that quality?

One advantage for cruise ships, which they pass along to their guests in a lower markup, is that wines may be bought duty-free, and ships do not pay U.S. federal or excise taxes. As a result, they can expand their affordable assortment of wines for guests. It also potentially opens up opportunities for you to meet a variety of cruise line price points and expectations.

Internet research will provide you with the names of all or most major cruise ship lines and cruise ship brokers. Wine placements with cruise ships can also ignite interest from an American importer and raise awareness for your wines with international cruise guests. Whether you are able to secure a place on a core list or only a limited time feature item, maximize the opportunity by using that exposure to springboard to the next break in the U.S. market. Your resourcefulness in pursuing an unconventional avenue demonstrates qualities that could make the difference with a potential mainstream importer.

* * *

Final Thoughts

In the course of my importing career, I have sold to large chains, smaller chains and a cruise ship line. In every instance, when I was in control of my own supply with a direct line to the retail buyer, I enjoyed greater success in the position of importer than if I abdicated control to a third-party or was removed from the transactions. The key to success are the following all-important points:

- *Relationships*—establishing and building rapport with a buyer who enjoys dealing with you
- *Being the decision maker*—having the ability to negotiate with the buyer to mutual advantage and seeing what is required to close the deal
- *Being in a position to respond rapidly to buyer's needs*—as their direct contact, there is no waiting for a broker or distributor, for whom this may not be a priority when there are so many demands made on their time and efforts for other products in their portfolios

In my experience with a large, national chain I sold to for several years, when I was also the distributor in my home-based state, the relationship deepened and I enjoyed even greater success.

I sold to several medium-sized chains with varying degrees of success, but I recall one less successful venture in particular. The chain had ordered their first container of four varieties of one private label brand, which was a good start both in terms of volume and the breadth of choice. It meant more options for the consumer and more 'facings' on the shelf. However, when the wine arrived every label was identical. There was no way to differentiate varieties, which was confusing for both customer and the retailer trying to stock shelves in each store from cases in their stockroom. Despite having submitted different labels to TTB for COLA, the winery decided it was cheaper to print them all the one color. Based on this one critical mistake, I did not receive a second order for this brand.

I also had the experience of selling to Disney Cruise Lines. Sales were never at a container level, but they brought in a range of very good quality wines from my portfolio for their cruises, which seemed to sell moderately well. This business was achieved through the efforts of my distributor in Florida and unfortunately I was discouraged from making a personal connection with the buyer, much to my brands' detriment. I accepted this too easily, believing that the distributor would look after my best interests. The wines were eventually dropped by Disney in favor of other suppliers for reasons that were never made known to me, but could have included incentives and a strong working relationship. In this case, since there was no relationship between Disney Cruise Lines and myself, any reason was sufficient to change out the selection.

The point of this chapter has been to encourage you to 'think outside the box.' Although your primary goal is to attract a reputable, enthusiastic importer who can devote time to brand building, your own goals are paramount in the process of achieving long lasting sales and distribution in the U.S. This may be realized through exploring the chain store, private label or cruise ship path, either to achieve your first sales or ultimately support your importer's efforts.

15

In for the Long Haul

U.S. wine laws may be cumbersome, outmoded and obstructive, but the U.S. wine industry is dynamic, innovative and quick to jump on trends. If the U.S. is an important commercial arena to you, then monitoring it and being ready to respond rapidly and appropriately to needs, changes, growth opportunities or a decline in sales is vital.

Staying Ahead of Demand

No matter what type of distribution avenues you have managed to establish in the U.S., there will always be times when you have to anticipate demand for your wines, and yet you are not in a position to drive it. This point is so important that it is worth repeating: *you will have to anticipate demand even though you are not in a position to drive it.* Although I have been talking a great deal about finding access to this market, forging your path and supporting your importer's efforts, the bottom line is that these are not your sales and you are not in control of your wine's destiny. However passionately you may feel about your obscure flagship wine, for example, or your twenty-year-old 17% alcohol red wine, rare as hen's teeth and selling for the equivalent of $70 a bottle in your home country, it is probably never going to be anything other than a novelty in the U.S., if purchased at all. You must listen to those on the ground with experience, or at least listen to their needs and respond accordingly, if U.S. distribution is important to your long range plans. Some of the issues driving volume, and demand for certain wines, will be the same as other countries, but if this is your first export venture, particularly in the U.S., consider where your wines might fit and what factors influence sales in the U.S.:

- **Price points**—in line with the competition or over-delivering for the quality

- **Demand for wines of your region**—on the leading edge of a new trend, or riding the wave of heightened demand

- **Demand for your wines in particular**—hitting a sweet spot in pricing, and finding that people are responding enthusiastically to the packaging or style

- **State by state distribution**—the number of state wholesalers your importer has established for your brand, which of the concentrated population regions have the wines, and whether distribution is growing

- **Future expectations for the wine's sales growth**—many factors could influence this, among them how you or your importer plan on increasing exposure, which markets you may open up, expansion of your importer's business, bringing new wines into the lineup, or discount program pricing

- **Ratings and reviews**—although this is less critical to a brand's success these days, diluted by online reviews, peer recommendations and available research, it is nonetheless a factor and with consistent high ratings comes increased exposure, recognition of the brand and resulting sales

- **Marketing**—your efforts to promote your brand through advertising, interviews, social media campaign and word of mouth will likely drive sales

- **Expansion into other foreign markets**—if you anticipate that the remaining production or a greater share of the vintage could go to expanded distribution into other markets, this needs to be communicated to your U.S. importer who may have earmarked the original production figures you gave him or her to new projects or increased demand. This is a tricky one, because you really don't want to slow momentum for wines on an upward trajectory in any country, nor do you wish to hinder the efforts of your U.S. importer by denying them wine volume they may have counted on for their own needs

In planning for demand, your importer will most likely be looking at their current needs, sufficient product to supply reorders and a cushion to allow for unexpected events. You cannot expect your importer to store, at their expense, excess inventory too far into the future for sales that may not materialize, so a balance of needs on both sides will have to be accommodated.

Staying ahead of demand means putting the market's needs ahead of your own in many respects, as long as you can see sales are continuing to rise and it makes fiscal sense. If your vineyard can produce wines that appeal to the U.S. palate and attract an importer and distribution in the first place, don't mess with success by attempting to introduce something the market isn't ready for, just because you have inventory waiting in tanks or barrels, or you feel it is more indicative of your personal winemaking style. Additionally, do not attempt to radically alter the current wines' styles either, especially if they have proven to work as they are.

Vintage Management

Your importer will often ask you what is new or "fresh" in your lineup. They could have been supplying the same vintage to their distributors for a prolonged period of time and want the next vintage as a way to stimulate renewed interest. Or because, unless the wine is a venerable, aged reserve, the prevailing thinking in the U.S. is that you should be on such-and-such vintage (especially whites) at a marked point in time.

How you respond to this will be affected by when harvest occurs in your region. In New Zealand, for example, a Sauvignon Blanc could conceivably be released in August and in the U.S. market in September, before California vineyards have even picked their grapes. But the release of a 2014 white in September 2014 is more of a novelty than a guideline as to when a wine should be released. However, if that same 2014 white is still available in September 2017, there are bound to be questions from vendors. It may be drinking beautifully, even better than before. Reviewers may even say "best from 2016" on their tasting notes. Nonetheless, distributors will still ask when the latest vintage is due for release.

There is much more latitude with regard to the vintage release of reds. Your Cabernet may have been aged two years in oak and then left a year in bottle before its release. Therefore, a 2012 wine can be a new release in late 2015. It could be such a tannic wine that a later release is anticipated and expected. But there are still some exceptions. A young, bright Grenache and a light, lively Beaujolais will generally be given little leeway because these are wines that will show best in their youth and their release is expected within narrow parameters.

The above is to illustrate that there is some play on either side of vintage expectations but, in general, the perception of a brand will be more favorable when there is regular turnover. This may run counter to your idea that you will require your importer to take all of one vintage before moving on to the next vintage. If you can manage inventory and sales effectively through other distribution, providing wines to your U.S. importer in concert with market demand will be advantageous.

Your wines may be enjoying routinely positive press for multiple vintages and selling well, but this is all the more reason that release timing of the next vintage should be an orchestrated part of your importer's overall plan. This keeps anticipation high. In fact, there are times when you are in a better position if you run out of a vintage, with the promise of the next release in days or weeks, than to still have one or more vintages in inventory when another arrives. Unless the previous vintage is a highly regarded icon that exceeds demand for the new vintage, your importer will be forced to discount remaining inventory.

Reorder Timing

Whether your customer is one importer, multiple importers or direct sales to chains cleared through their own importers, the considerations of reorder timing will be the same. In addition to juggling market factors and conditions, there are logistical questions in the event of any order:

- Is the wine bottled?
- Do you have to book into a bottling queue?
- Is the wine labeled?
- Will the printer be able to accommodate your schedule?
- Has the label changed to the extent that it will require a new COLA (Certificate of Label Approval)?
- Is the wine ready to be released?
- Is your winery, or the contracted winery, staffed to handle the order in an efficient timetable?
- Are shipping schedules backed up from your country or region, and do they require advance booking?

The length of time the wine will take on the water and overland are of the same importance as the first time the wine was introduced. Except that this time there are more people counting on your customers and, potentially, more to lose if you are unable to deliver as promised. Anticipation is one thing, but losing sales that cannot be recovered could be a catastrophe, both for you and your importer.

Long Term Goal Planning

I recommend asking for very little of your importer in terms of concrete commitments and quantifiable goals in the early stages of distribution in the U.S. because, for most brands, it is a time of establishing a new line without any previous historical reference or relevant indication of sales volume. It will be a nascent venture for both your brand and your importer. Even if your brand has been in the market previously, many factors will have changed in the interim, including the economy, exchange rates and evolving tastes. You cannot rely on what you sold before or where you sold it as a barometer for sales with your new importer. However, as time advances, whether this is after the first year or the first container, you will most definitely have a better sense of what your brand and your importer are capable of achieving. It is at this stage that it is reasonable to ask for goals from the importer and express your own expectations. When you first began exporting, it was for a variety of reasons, including possibly taking up the slack in inventory, seeking perceived status for your wines, or discovering whether penetrating this market was possible. None of these reasons are unusual or wrong but now you have to make business decisions based on a rational and viable model for the future.

- Do anticipated allocations to the U.S. deplete your production or do you need to find distribution elsewhere?
- Do you need to ramp up or scale back vineyard production?
- Is one U.S. importer enough or is it time to add more (assuming that existing sales will attract others)?
- What are your importer's articulated goals for your brand and are they aligned with your own?
- What logical expectations can you have of your importer, based on current sales and projections, and their geographical reach and resources?

This is a good time to discuss with your importer the performance of the distributors they have appointed. Based on their conversations, observations and measurable sales:

- Which distributors are performing as expected?
- Which ones are under performing and what can be done, or is being done, about them?
- Have any distributors expressed opinions on anything new or different they would like to see in their marketplace?
- Do the individual distributors have their own projections for the future of your brand in their region based on, for example, volume, sales team enthusiasm, what is working, what is not, and whether their business model and/or sales area is expanding?

It is also a time to evaluate pricing, positioning and prospects, considering what factors have influenced your brand's sales and progress throughout the previous year. Whether the goals are defined on spreadsheets with precise facts and figures or conveyed verbally, the explicit and quantifiable must be married with the indeterminate and idiosyncratic. These goals and objectives are not made in a vacuum, but must also be considered alongside the personality and potential of your importer, and the capricious nature of the wine consuming public. In this equation, it is up to you to deliver as promised in terms of the quality and integrity of your wines and other factors within your control. You cannot expect your importer to live up to their end of the bargain if you suddenly change the rules in the middle of the game.

Social Media

Social media, by which I mean online or web based community interaction in many different forms, is now an integral part of our lives and impacts our businesses. I would be remiss if I did not at least devote a section to acknowledge its impact on wine marketing. This does not necessarily mean you are in the least bit interested in tweeting, blogging, having conversations on Google+ or posting pictures to Instagram, but I was reminded very recently that everyone in the world is connected in ways we never imagined. A friend of mine who loves to read obscure literary books discovered a kindred spirit in a sheep herder in the Cumbrian Fells of England, who tweets about daily life while he works and loves the same books. You never know where or when you will find that kindred spirit who discovers a love for your wine.

If this does not apply to you or you don't have much interest in social media as a way to communicate with your customer, then at least I have introduced you to the subject and 'connected' you to the available technology.

Social media marketing may be something your importer is doing and you can follow their efforts. Or, if your winery is large enough, perhaps you have a marketing specialist or consultant who can devote time to promoting your brand. If so, you may want to provide input or be involved in directing the brand's message.

There are so many different marketing technology options now, and most likely something else will have come along by the time you read this book, but they are not all relevant to your situation, can be too time consuming for the ROI (return on investment) and may not suit your personal style. If you enjoy photography and take beautiful photos of your vineyard and the winemaking process, then Instagram and Pinterest may be of interest to you, but generally there is little time for any social media other than directed marketing, if at all. So my suggestions, for you or your importer, are limited to what I consider a top few.

Facebook
Although clearly a social media outlet for recreational posting and staying in touch with friends and family, having a business page devoted to your brand is a medium where you can post about the latest happenings in the vineyard, new releases, breaking award news and anything you feel would interest your fans. When someone 'likes' your page, they are not only indicating a preference for your product or content, but demonstrating to their friends that they favor your brand. This impacts their friends in a personal recommendation, which may lead to more 'likes' and an expansion of recognition for your brand.

A dynamic web page can function in a similar way in terms of traffic, but driving traffic to your website is much harder.

Twitter
An interactive way to communicate or market your product or business in quick bursts. It is a service that allows communication in 140 characters or less, with the ability to include links to articles, websites (your own, for example) and news and attach photos. I find it is an easy and manageable way to catch up on wine related news or provide my own links when I have limited time. As with all social media, it is a personal choice and you must decide if it suits your personality or style. Incorporated with other media, such as Facebook or a blog, it is another effective means to provide a branding tie-in and capitalize on your marketing efforts or specific promotions, such as a contest, new release or event.

LinkedIn

From my frequent mentions of LinkedIn, it is easy to gather that I consider this to be a highly effective tool in wine business. However, it is only one tool and may best be utilized as you are seeking importing and distribution and establishing your business rather than an ongoing outlet. I certainly recommend joining the LinkedIn community to set up a profile and establish an identity, connecting with people who may be helpful resources and contacts, especially since so many of the groups originated in the U.S.

YouTube

Despite You Tube's user's propensity for cute animal videos or people behaving badly, there is a big business side to You Tube that can capture your vineyard, winery or brand's individual character if your personality or inclination lends itself to making videos. There are a myriad of subjects, but they could include showcasing vineyard terroir, winemaking techniques, bud burst, harvest, release of wines, and producer's vision for his or her wines. These can be standalone videos or embedded in your website. It may be quite an ambitious and far-reaching project if you have a small vineyard in a remote region of Italy, but as a worthwhile social media outlet, it should have a mention.

Blog

Creating a blog is free on sites such as Word Press. They are easy to set up and maintain. The key to a potentially successful and well-read blog is to focus on a theme. In your case it is simple: the vineyard and the wines. In my case it is wine business. Although I'm not the best example of keeping up with regular blog posts, they can be consistent sources of content for interested consumers and a way to promote your wines without saying, "Buy my wine." Blogs should either be embedded in or linked to your website.

QR Codes

FIGURE 22   Social media changes (percent of online adults who use the following social media services, by year*)

Service	2012	2013	2014
Facebook	67%	71%	71%
LinkedIn	20%	22%	28%
Pinterest	15%	21%	28%
Instagram	13%	17%	26%
Twitter	16%	18%	23%

* Pew Research Center, Internet Project Survey. 2012–2014 data collected September 11–14 and September 18–21, 2014. N = 1,597 Internet users ages 18 and older.

This isn't strictly speaking, social media, but it certainly can be used to engage the consumer and is actually one form of media marketing that you can easily adopt, irrespective of whether you enjoy or feel capable of blogging, tweeting, and so on. Because of marketing misuse or abuse, QR (quick response) codes seem to be undergoing some decline as of this writing, but I believe they still have value if used correctly. They are surprisingly easy and relatively inexpensive to purchase and can be tailored to a variety of uses, such as contests, tasting notes, videos and upcoming releases or events. You will think of many more marketing tools that suit your own environment and brand assets.

Remember to think of your target consumer as a fan or a friend of the brand. They have taken the time to scan the code because they are interested to learn more. Don't just direct them to your static website or a shopping cart. The former is boring and the latter could be interpreted as offensive. They have already purchased your wine or are contemplating doing so. Make this a fun and informational experience. Have helpful and specific food and wine pairings for this wine, show tasting notes that give far more than what can fit on the bottle, or even a video where the winemaker is talking about vintage and this wine. If you have a contest, indicate that on the label itself, so that they know what to expect if they scan the QR code.

If you do go to the trouble of printing a QR code and establishing usable content, make sure it is readable by a scanner before it goes on the label.

Keys to Social Media Success

- Continue to update content regularly. It may be something small on Facebook or Twitter, but it will keep fans and followers coming back to see what's new and your brand at the forefront of their minds.

- Remember that content, not a sales pitch, is what you want to promote. The sales pitch is inherent in the marketing, but it will turn people off if you are not offering informational value and a sense of connection.

- Acknowledge mentions of your wine or RTs (retweets) of your own tweets on Twitter with a thank you. It not only says you appreciate their attention, but strengthens the relationship. RT the positive comments people make about your wine and their experience.

- Don't feel you have to auto-follow everyone on Twitter who follows you. This is your medium to shape your experience. Don't lose sight of your objective: to market your wines through engagement. People follow those they are interested in, and you should do the same. If those interests converge, then following them is a natural extension.

- Whatever social media avenue you choose, make sure you have those icons on your website or blog, to make it easier for people to tweet, follow, 'like' or link.

* * *

Final Thoughts

In this section, I'd like to relate two experiences with wines that serve as cautionary tales for any brand owner and make excellent examples of shortsighted thinking.

First Case Study

Many years ago, I imported a cool climate, unoaked Chardonnay with luscious, tropical fruit characters and rich mouth feel. It was very different from Chardonnays of that era but held great appeal for a distributor in New York who ordered consistently large volume.

One day, I received an angry phone call from that same distributor asking why I had shipped him entirely different wines on the last order. I knew nothing of any 'switch', but presumed something had happened to the wine during storage or transport. Although I stored the wine in temperature controlled conditions, I asked the warehouse to pull bottle samples from different cases and send them to me. The evidence was clear. The wine was perfectly fine, but some of the bottles contained wine that was unoaked, fruit-driven, and as expected, and others had clearly spent some time in French oak. They were still very good, but nothing like the style the distributor wanted.

When I called the winery owner, he readily admitted the changes he had made in the wine's processing. He didn't think it was important to tell me and assumed I would like the more expensively aged wine. Not only was this a critical mistake, but I lost my good reputation and all further business with the New York distributor.

Second Case Study
A number of years later, I imported a brand that was suddenly enormously popular as a result of consistently high ratings and a ranking in the Top 100 Wines of the Year in Wine Spectator. Demand for this winery's wines soared with each new vintage. This was a family-owned vineyard with fairly extensive plantings, but production couldn't keep up. They made a decision to source grapes from other vineyards to make a wine that closely matched the original wine, but not tell anyone that it was a different bottling, and not even from the supplier's own vineyard. This was discovered by one of the brand's competitors who immediately alerted media outlets, and the resulting publicity was disastrous. While the brand owner maintained that they had not altered the wine's essential qualities and hadn't meant to deceive anyone, the damage was done. The brand did eventually recover but not for several years and never to its former status.

The point to these stories is that any alterations you consider to your line should be disclosed to and discussed with your importer. Trends shift and it might be the right time for a French oak aged Chardonnay, or consumers could be more interested in a well-priced, good wine than whether it was a second bottling, but the response will never be positive if the information is only disclosed after the fact. Keeping lines of communication open and viewing your importer as a partner is one key to developing your export business.

Conclusion

Following the publication of my first book, *How to Import Wine—An Insider's Guide,* a number of people outside the United States asked me if I was planning to write a book to educate them on the process to enter this market. I was surprised by their inquiries because I thought my original book answered many of these questions. Later, I realized that although it gave a view of the wine business world inside the U.S., it stopped short of opening the door and allowing the foreign supplier to step through. This book attempts to deliver a key to the door, or at least some options for opening it. All the answers are not in this book. You will rarely, if ever, find all the answers in one book on any subject. But it is my sincere attempt to share my thoughts, knowledge and experience with you, in the hope that you find something of value. As with the first book, I have offered concrete guidelines amid the questions you must ask yourself about your wines and the type of business you wish to pursue. My own examples, as was pointed out to me after the first book, tend towards "painful" lessons, but I use these to demonstrate the need to arm yourself with resources and education, something I did not have access to at the time. In doing so, you will avoid many of the same mistakes. Similarly, when I focus on some of the less positive personalities in this business it is as illustrations of conduct that runs contrary to establishing good relationships, the cornerstone of wine sales. On the other hand, I have been privileged to encounter and become good friends with a large circle of fun, interesting, generous, goodhearted people who have enriched my life and created warm, lasting memories. My experiences in this industry over the past twenty-three years have been overwhelmingly positive.

The most recent statistics for wine sales tell a very optimistic story for wine demand in this country, for both domestic and imported wine. Consumption and sales across the board have set records and with the economy recovering at a steady pace there is no reason to believe this demand won't continue. While competition may be vigorous, it is still a vital and dynamic market with a growing population and increasingly more adventurous wine drinkers.

My final advice to you is to be genuine in your relationships and encounters. Show how much you love your wines. Passion is infectious.

I wish you every success in attracting representation for your wines and accomplishing your export goals.

Foreign Trade Organizations
(partial list)

www.italtrade.com

www.bordeaux.com

www.vins-bourgogne

www.winesofchile.org

www.wineaustralia.com

www.nzwine.com

www.wineofczechrepublic.cz/en/

www.germanwineusa.com

www.winesofargentina.org

www.wosa.co.za

www.portugal.org

Index

Symbols

21st Amendment 10, 17

A

accolades 40. *See also* awards
age groups 9. *See also* Millennials
agents 4, 54
Alcohol and Tobacco Tax and Trade Bureau (TTB) 4, 6, 21, 74, 89
  changes to requirements 92
Alcoholic Beverage Control (ABC) 12–13
allocation 70
American Source Letter 85
Animal and Plant Health Inspection Service (APHIS) 111
Appointment Letter. *See* American Source Letter
awards 56, 103. *See also* accolades

B

background checking 71
barcodes 95

bill-backs 166
Bill of Lading 115
  non-negotiable 117
bills of parcel. *See* packing lists
blogging 135, 196
brand label 94
brand launch 125
brand representatives 43
brochures and printed background materials 99
brokers. *See also* agents
  benefits of 133
  costs of 133–134
  exporter's relationship with 55
  functions of 54–55
budgets 156–157
buyers
  expectations of 159–161, 166
  relationships with 186–187
  retail chains 57
by-the-glass programs 125, 140
  pitfalls of 141

C

California 12
case cards 105
cellar door visits 57–59

Certificate of Label Approval
(COLA) 4, 89
  common corrections 92
  online application 92-93
  turnaround time 93
China xv
commercial invoices 115
compliance importers 26-27
consolidations 113
consumer tastings 172, 175-176
containers 112
  dry 112
  insulated 112
  refrigerated. *See* reefers
contracts 77-78
  forward 81
Control states 11, 17
  brokers in 133
Cost, Insurance and Freight
(CIF) 108
cruise ships 184
  core list 184
  markup 185
  requirements for accepting
   wines 184
currency 80. *See also* exchange
 rates
customer receipts. *See* packing lists
customs clearance 4-5

D

delivery dockets. *See* packing lists
delivery lists. *See* packing lists
demand 189-191
  pricing 121
depletion reports 176-178
dessert wines 170
Direct Import (DI) 181-182
discounts 109, 125, 127
  for samples 78-79
distribution process 137
distributors. *See also* wholesalers
  as importers 5
  evaluation of 193-194
  markup 124-125
  meaning of 4
  what importers want in 132
  wine sampling 138
dockets. *See* packing lists
dry containers 112

E

emails 7, 37-38
ex-cellars. *See* ex-works (EXW)
exchange rates 55, 80-81, 121
export agents. *See* agents, brokers
export brokers. *See* brokers
ex-works (EXW) 109

F

Facebook 195
Federal Basic Permit 26
financial stability 36
first year volume 69-70
Food and Drug Administration
(FDA) 75-77, 114-115
foreign markets 190
foreign trade organizations 44
forward contracts 81
four-tier system 133
Franchise states 17-18
Free on Board (FOB) 108, 122
freight forwarders 112
Full Container Load (FCL) 113, 123

G

geographical reach 35
Georgia (state) 18, 20
glass pour programs. *See* by-the-
  glass programs
goals
  long-term 193-194

short-term 81–82, 147–148
government
  as wholesaler and retailer 11–12
  intervention in sales 17. *See also* Control states
  sponsoring foreign trade organizations 44
  sponsoring trade events 41–42
government warnings. *See* health warning statements
grocery stores 182–183
  banned wine sales in 19

H

health warning statements 74–75, 91–92
How to Import Wine: An Insider's Guide xvi, 3, 201
hybrid supplier-importer business 24

I

importers
  as distributors 5, 124
  compliance 26–27
  how to find 37
  independent 23
  markup 123–124
  meaning of 4
  national 65–66
  regional 67
  relationship with suppliers 35, 63–64, 143–145
  reverse search 47–48
  role of 30–31
  things to look for in 34–37
Importer's Basic Permit 29. *See also* importing licenses
importing
  licenses 21
  national vs. regional 65
importing licenses 21

incentives 127, 139
  launch or pre-sell 140
  ongoing off-premise 141
  ongoing on-premise 141
initial volume. *See* first year volume
insulated containers 112
International Carrier Terms (Incoterms) 108
Internet 46–47, 47. *See also* social media
invoices 114
  commercial 115
  tax 115

L

labels
  approval. *See* Certificate of Label Approval (COLA)
  brand 94
  examples of 30–33, 94–96
  printing 92
  private 182–183
  rejection 93
  requirements 90–92
  translating 96
  warnings. *See* health warning statements
language barriers 54. *See also* translations
Less than Container Load (LCL) 113, 123
letter of intent 29
letters. *See* letter of intent
licenses. *See* importing licenses
LinkedIn 7, 48, 196–197
long-term goals 193–194

M

marketing 99, 190
market visits 148. *See also* sales calls
  budget 156
  events 169

market visits (continued)
  local customs 165–167
  planning 152
  protocol 164–165
  timing 148–149
markups
  cruise ship 185
  distributor 124
  importer 123–124
  restaurant 183
  retail 124
"milk run" accounts 164
Millennials xvi, xviii, 9
misconceptions 3–7
Moët Hennessy 48
myths 3–7

N

national importers. *See* national representation
national representation 65
net profit 79
non-negotiable Bill of Lading 117

O

off-premise
  incentives 141–142
  sales 140
on-premise
  incentives 141–142
  sales 140

P

packaging slips. *See* packing lists
packing lists 115
pallets 110
payment terms 68
per capita consumption 16
permits. *See* Federal Basic Permit, Importer's Basic Permit

personality 178
  fit for partnerships 35, 63–65
  of winemaker 160
placement reports 176
Point of Sale (POS) material 99
positioning 124
pre-selling 136
presentations
  at sales meetings 167–168
  at wine dinners 170–171
pricing 81, 119–122
  based on awards or demand 121
  broker's role in 55–56
  importer's role in 31
prior notice 114
private labels 182–183
profit margins 22, 123, 181
Prohibition 10, 17
publications 134
  The Wine Advocate xvii, 134
  Wine Enthusiast 134–136
  Wine Spectator xvii, 134–136
  Wine & Spirits 134–135
purchase orders 97–99

Q

QR codes 196–197

R

ratings 56, 103, 135–136, 190
  value of xvii, 9
reefers 112
refrigerated containers. *See* reefers
regional importers 67–68
relationships
  importer-supplier 34, 63–64, 143–145
  with brokers 55
  with buyers 186–187
reorders 192
reports

depletion 177–178
placement 176
representation
  national. *See* national representation
restaurants. *See also* by-the-glass programs
  markup 183
  on-premise incentives 139
  private labels 183
  selling wine to 125
retail chains 180
  buyers from 57
  importers for 57, 181
  markup 124
  types of 180
reverse importer search 47
reviews. *See* ratings, publications

S

sales calls 157–158
  customs 165–166
sales meetings 167–168
samples 73
  allowance 78
  bottle requirements 74
  cost to clear 5
  for wholesalers/distributors 138
  pre-selling 136
  purposes of 79
  submitting to publications 134–136
  who can send 4
Sea Waybill Express Release 117
shelf talkers 104
shipping 109
  size and weights 109
shipping lists. *See* packing lists
short-term goals 81–82, 147–148
social media xviii, 8, 194–198
suppliers
  relationship with importers 35, 63

T

tasting notes 99
tasting rooms
  visits to 57–59
tastings
  consumer. *See* consumer tastings
taxes
  variation between states 122
tax invoice 115
thermal blankets 112
thermal containers. *See* insulated containers
The Wine Advocate xvii, 134
three-tier system
  controversy and difficulty of 121–122
  effects on pricing 80
  examples of 11, 57
  in unconventional markets 179–181
  structure of 10
Tied-House laws 12–13
trade events 7, 40–44
  government-sponsored 41–42
  independent 41
trade tastings 172
  distributors 172–174
  independent 174–175
  results of 175
translations 37, 54, 96, 99
transportation
  of wine. *See* shipping
  within United States 156–157
TTB. *See* Alcohol and Tobacco Tax and Trade Bureau (TTB)
Twitter 195, 198
two-tier system 11

U

unaccompanied wine 4
United States Department of Agriculture (USDA) 111
United States wine market xvi
  current influences on 8–9
  diversity of 3, 13, 122, 132, 154
unpacking notes. *See* packing lists
U.S. Customs and Border Protection 74, 111, 114. *See also* customs clearance

V

vineyards
  visits to 57–59
vintages
  management of 191–192
  variations 99
Vinum Magazine 56
visits
  to cellar doors or tasting rooms 57
  to U.S. wine market. *See* market visits
volume
  first year 69–70
  top states by 15

W

warnings. *See* health warning statements
websites 46, 181
  marketing use 99
wholesalers. *See also* distributors
  meaning of 4, 6
  overhead costs 124
  sales volume 124
  wine sampling 138
wine dinners 169
  speaking at 171
Wine Enthusiast 134–136
wine fairs 40–44
wineries
  visits to 57–59
Wine Spectator xvii, 134–136
Wine & Spirits 134–135
wood packing materials (WPM) 111

Y

Yellow Tail 24
YouTube 196

The Wine Business Library

ORGANIC WINE: A MARKETER'S GUIDE
Béatrice Cointreau

Building on detailed case studies, Cointreau presents an exhaustive analysis of global production and market trends, and provides clear insights on how to position one's product to the best effect.

$29.95
ISBN 978-1935879633
Pub Date: October 1, 2015
Paperback, 6 x 9 inches, 200 pp., graphs and charts

WINE MARKETING & SALES, 2ND EDITION
Paul Wagner, Janeen Olsen, Ph.D., and Liz Thach, Ph.D, foreword by Robert Mondavi

This completely revised and updated edition of the bestselling book puts new, practical, and powerful strategies into the hands of veteran brand managers and marketing professionals, and the vast bank of wine marketing knowledge within reach of the nascent winery owner.

$75.00
ISBN 978-1-934259-25-2
Hardcover, 7 x 10 inches, 400 pp., illustrations and fully indexed

WINE BUSINESS CASE STUDIES: THIRTEEN CASES FROM THE REAL WORLD OF WINE BUSINESS MANAGEMENT
Pierre Mora, Editor

Published in association with the Bordeaux College of Business, this book applies business pedagogy's powerful learning tool to the unique challenges of wine business management. *Wine Business Case Studies* is written by an international group of respected wine business scholars.

$30.00
ISBN 978-1-935879-71-8
Paperback, 8.5 x 11 inches, 300 pp., graphs and charts

THE BUSINESS OF WINEMAKING
Jeffrey L. Lamy

Places all facets of the wine business in perspective for investors, owners, and anyone else who is interested in how the wine business operates.

$45.00
ISBN 978-1-935879-65-7
Paperback, 7 x 10 inches, 360 pp., 250 illustrations, charts, graphs, and fully indexed

WINE MARKETING ONLINE
Brue McGechan

The whole wired realm of wine marketing is revealed in this encyclopedic yet readable and easy-to-follow guide.

$29.95
ISBN 978-1-935879-87-9
Paperback, 6 x 9 inches, 418 pp., illustrations and fully indexed

HOW TO LAUNCH YOUR WINE CAREER
Liz Thach, Ph.D. & Brian D'Emilio, foreword by Michael Mondavi

Career coaching from two of wine's most respected professionals and scores of industry icons like winemaker Heidi Barrett and writer James Laube of the *Wine Spectator*.

$29.95
ISBN 978-1-934259-06-1
Paperback, 6 x 9 inches, 354 pp., fully indexed

BOARDANDBENCH.COM

The Viticulture and Enology Library

CONCEPTS IN WINE TECHNOLOGY, SMALL WINERY OPERATIONS
Yair Margalit, Ph.D.

Revised and updated, this detailed how-to guide, written by physical chemist and winemaker Yair Margalit, is organized in the sequence of winemaking, and is both an excellent text for the classroom and a concise guide for the practicing winemaker.

$40.00
ISBN 978-1-935879-80-0
Hardcover, 7 x 10 inches, 320 pp., illustrations, charts, graphs, and fully indexed

WINE FAULTS: CAUSES, EFFECTS, CURES
John Hudelson, Ph.D., foreword by John Buechsenstein

A precise and comprehensive description of the problems encountered at times by all winemakers and wine judges. Every microbial infection found in today's wineries is fully described and arrayed in full-color slides.

$39.95
ISBN 978-1-934259-63-4
Paperback, 8.5 x 11 inches, 96 pp., full-color illustrations and fully indexed

CONCEPTS IN WINE CHEMISTRY, 3RD EDITION
Yair Margalit, Ph.D.

In this new edition of his classic text, Yair Margalit gives complete and current pictures of the basic and advanced science behind the biochemistry of vilification, making the updated *Concepts in Wine Chemistry* the broadest and most meticulous book on the topic in print.

$89.95
ISBN 978-1-935879-81-7
Hardcover, 7 x 10 inches, 550 pp., illustrations, charts, graphs, and fully indexed

BIODYNAMIC WINE, DEMYSTIFIED
Nicholas Joly, foreword by Mike Benziger & Joshua Greene

Joly shares the core philosophy behind biodynamic viticulture and explains why the use of foreign substances disrupt vineyard ecology and are ultimately counterproductive to a wine's best, consistent expression.

$24.95
ISBN 978-1-934259-02-3
Paperback, 6 x 9 inches, 180 pp., color plates and fully indexed

UNDERSTANDING WINE TECHNOLOGY, 3RD EDITION
David Bird, foreword by Hugh Johnson

This completely revised and updated edition deciphers all the new scientific advances that have cropped up in the last several years and conveys them in Bird's typically clear and plainspoken style.

$44.95
ISBN 978-1-934259-60-3
Paperback, 6 x 8 inches, 328 pp., full-color illustrations, charts, and fully indexed

VIEW FROM THE VINEYARD: A PRACTICAL GUIDE TO SUSTAINABLE WINEGRAPE GROWING
Clifford P. Ohmart, Ph.D.

This comprehensive examination of the subject provides the farmer with a path to a sustainable vineyard and concludes with a self-assessment guide in which growers can easily track their progress.

$34.95
ISBN 978-1935879909
Hardcover, 7 x 10 inches, 240 pp., color and fully indexed

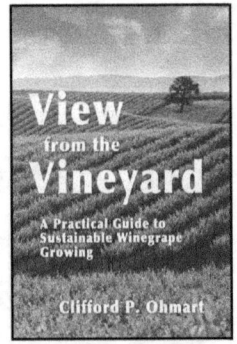

BOARDANDBENCH.COM

www.ingramcontent.com/pod-product-compliance
Lightning Source LLC
Chambersburg PA
CBHW070352240426
43671CB00013BA/2470